PRINCETON THEOLOGICAL MONOGRAPH SERIES

Dikran Y. Hadidian

General Editor

7

SAINTS: VISIBLE, ORDERLY AND CATHOLIC

The Congregational Idea of the Church

Alfred Dye, Minister of the Gospel
Robert Mackintosh: Theologian of Integrity
God our Father
The Great Debate: Calvinism, Arminianism and
      Salvation
Church Planting: A Study of Westmorland
      Nonconformity
Theology in Turmoil: The roots, course and
      significance of the conservative-liberal
      debate in modern theology
Defending and Declaring the Faith: Some
      Scottish examples 1860-1920 (forthcoming)

SAINTS:

VISIBLE, ORDERLY AND CATHOLIC

The Congregational Idea of the Church

ALAN P.F. SELL

PICKWICK PUBLICATIONS
Allison Park, Pennsyvania

First published in 1986 by
The World Alliance of Reformed Churches,
150 route de Ferney, 1211 Geneva 20, Switzerland

and by
Pickwick Publications
4137 Timberlane Drive
Allison Park, PA 15101, USA

Library of Congress Cataloging in Publication Data

Sell, Alan P.F.
  Saints—visible, orderly and catholic.
  (Princeton theological monograph series ; 7)
  Includes index
  1. Congregationalism. I. Title. II. Series.
  BX7231.2.S44 1986   285.8   86-9457
  ISBN 0-915138-89-1

Contents

Preface

The unanimous verdict of text books of systematic theology is that there are three main types of church order: the episcopal, the presbyterial and the congregational. In the present ecumenical climate there is a tendency for Christians from all three traditions to draw closer together: indeed, in some places united churches have been established which incorporate elements of all three ecclesiologies. In Britain the distinctions were long-standing, and the road to reunion has been correspondingly winding. Nevertheless in 1972, in the first trans-confessional union in England and Wales since the Reformation, the English Presbyterians and the majority of the English and English-speaking Welsh Congregationalists came together to form the United Reformed Church.

In this book I attempt to trace the development of the congregational idea of the Church from its early expressions in England and America to the formation of the United Reformed Church. For what idea of the Church have Congregationalists stood, and what has become of their idea now that many of them have united with Presbyterians? In pursuing this theme I hope to remind past and future members of the United Reformed Church of an important and challenging part of their heritage; and I hope to raise points for discussion by the world-wide Reformed family, for the World Alliance of Reformed Churches is the result of the union in 1970 of the World Presbyterian Alliance with the International

Congregational Council. There are welcome signs that members of other Christian communions are being encouraged to reflect upon the ecumenical implications of Congregational catholicity. Thus, for example, the report of the 1970-77 bilateral dialogue between the Roman Catholic Secretariat for Promoting Christian Unity and the World Alliance of Reformed Churches, The Presence of Christ in Church and World, states that 'It is only by participating in the local community that we share in the life of the universal Church.' An account of the ecclesiological thinking of those for whom this insight has been a major part of their raison d'être would seem to be timely.

My first adventures in the field of comparative ecclesiology were undertaken at the age of fourteen. The result was that I became a Congregationalist by conviction, sensing that the congregational idea of the Church was of real importance. I now rejoice that the essential ingredients of visible sainthood, orderliness and catholicity have been preserved in the declared position of the United Reformed Church - though I suspect that in recent years we have paid more attention to orderliness and catholicity than to sainthood as such.

My publisher and I wish to thank the Free Church Federal Council for a generous grant towards the cost of publishing this volume. Thanks are also due to my secretary, Miss Dori Veiga for her careful work in preparing the text for printing.

It would have been foolhardy to have written on this theme without subjecting myself to the kindly and penetrating criticism of Dr. Geoffrey F. Nuttall. Indeed, on many occasions Dr. Nuttall has encouraged and instructed me when I have ventured into the

field of dissenting history. As a small token
of appreciation and affection I dedicate this
book to one who is both the foremost student
of the visible saints and, more importantly, a
visible saint himself.

Alan P.F. Sell
World Alliance of Reformed Churches,
Geneva
1986

1. Introduction

'Congregationalism', according to a current dictionary definition, 'is that form of Church polity which rests on the independence and autonomy of each local church.'[1] It would be difficult to make the thing defined sound less exciting, or worth dying for. Despite the fact that many Congregationalists over the years would have accepted the definition, the emphasis is wrongly placed. The suggestion is that 'Congregationalism' primarily denotes one among a number of churchly structures to be found within Christendom. Clearly, in a sense, it does; but three points require to be made.

First, Congregationalism did not emerge because certain Christians devised a church order which was to them preferable to any other. To suppose otherwise is to take too constitutionalist, and manward, a view of the matter. Rather, Congregationalism represents one way of responding to the conviction that by the Holy Spirit God calls his people to himself, and grafts them into his family. The polity is the response to God's redemptive initiative. If God is sovereign in salvation, how can he fail to be sovereign in the Church? If Christ is the Lord of life, can he be other than Lord of the Church which is his body? 'Independency,' wrote A.M. Fairbairn, 'apart from its religious basis and ideal, is at once mean and impotent, impracticable and visionary.

Our fathers held that legislation, civil or
ecclesiastical, could not create a church;
conversion and converted men alone could...In
His Church Christ did not reign while officials governed;He both governed and reigned.'[2]
Our fathers believed that their corporate,
covenanted life was their response to what God
had done for them in Christ; and the polity
which resulted from this conviction was their
attempt to realise Christ's Lordship in matters ecclesiastical.

Secondly, at its best Congregationalism has
never regarded itself as being one churchly
way among many. It has been happy to own that
its catholic understanding of the nature of
the Church has been shared by many who have
not been denominationally labelled 'Congregationalist.' Indeed, this very fact has on more
than one occasion prompted disquiet on the
part of Congregationalists when the denomina-
tionalist flag has been waved. Again, this
non-sectarian stance has puzzled members of
other Christian communions, and it must be
confessed that their puzzlement has by no
means dissolved when more idiosyncratic and
unrepresentative Congregationalists have positively rejoiced in vagueness <u>vis à vis</u> organisation, liturgy, and even fundamental
Christian doctrines. Nevertheless the claim is
- and it was never more bluntly (some would
say tendentiously) expressed than by Robert
Mackintosh - that 'Christianity as a polity,
when trimmed of superfluous fat and reduced to
its innermost essence, is Congregationalism.'[3]
We should be in error were we to suppose that
there is implicit here the arrogant claim that
empirical Congregationalism <u>attains</u> its high
ideal.

Thirdly, as to the terms 'independence' and
'autonomy': it cannot be denied that the idea

of the saints gathered is fundamental to Congregationalism. Congregational church members are saints; that is, they are Christians. They have, by grace, responded to grace, and they are challenged to a godly, empowered, walk. And they are gathered; they are a fellowship of people. Churchmanship is inescapable. To be in Christ is to be of his people. If, as P.T. Forsyth declared, Congregationalism's freedom is a founded freedom,[4] then surely its sainthood is a grounded sainthood. It is earthed. It is not that of the individualistic mystic. The saints are gathered by, and under, Christ. They meet in his name.[5] _Together_ they comprise that corporate priesthood of believers whose members enjoy direct access to the Head.

The question what else needs to obtain for a local gathering to be a church is one which has exercised, and sometimes divided, Congregationalists. It is a question which lays bare the fact that Congregational ecclesiology is not the product of one mind or of one group. What we find is an oscillation between Reformed and Anabaptist emphases in Congregationalism's roots.[6] But neither emphases (the term 'party' is too strong) at its best equated 'independency' with 'isolationism.' If on occasion Congregationalists have turned to Ignatius's remark, 'where Jesus Christ is, there is the catholic church,'[7] by way of justifying their independence (even if they have tended not to mention the importance of the bishop, and the reverence due to deacons to which Ignatius refers in the same paragraph!), at other times they have endorsed Tertullian's attitude towards wider expressions of Catholicity: 'how worthy a thing is this, that, under the auspices of faith, men should congregate from all quarters to Christ! "See, how

good and how enjoyable for brethren to dwell
in unity!"'[8]

A final preliminary consideration emerges
when the dictionary immediately proceeds to
say that Congregationalism 'professes to represent the principle of democracy in Church
government, a polity which is held to follow
from its fundamental belief in Christ as the
sole head of His Church.' It goes without
saying that our modern 'one man, one vote'
ideas of democracy are anachronistic when
applied to Congregationalism's founding fathers. Hence the oft-repeated protest that Congregationalism seeks to be a christocracy,
whose objective is unanimity in Christ and not
simply 'majority rule.' Presumably, when the
saints are most truly saints the terms
'christocratic' and 'democratic' are synony-
mous - or, at least, they are the concave and
convex of the same lens.[9]

Our aim is to make good the claims we have
somewhat dogmatically made, by reference to
the course of Congregational history. Our gaze
will resolutely - even narrowly - be fixed upon the question, 'How have Congregationalists
understood the nature of the Church?' We shall
confine our attention to those who have been
labelled 'Congregationalist.' This is not to
deny the polity to Baptists, to the Pente-
costals of the Assemblies of God, and to others. But none have explored the tensions implicit in the attempt to honour both independence and catholicity more fully than the Congregationalists with a capital 'C'. In stick-
ing to our last we shall not, except inciden-
tally and by implication, pursue such fascinating cognate questions as the nature of
ministry, of the sacraments, or of religious
establishment. On this last point our article,
'Dubious Establishment? A neglected ecclesiol-

ogical testimony', <u>Mid-Stream</u> XXIV, no.1, 1985, may be consulted.

Similarly, we shall not examine in detail the intriguing question of the overall ethos of Congregationalism. This would take us too far into such questions as the relation of Spirit and Word, law and liberty. It would entail a thorough consideration of Congregationalism's roots in continental anabaptism and Calvinism - on which fascinating theme P.T. Forsyth's <u>Faith, Freedom and the Future</u> remains a most stimulating introduction. Ours, to repeat, is the narrower task of displaying and examining Congregational views as to the nature of the Church.

In connection with this last point we shall maintain the contemporary relevance of our study. It is a pastoral as well as an ecclesiological relevance. In 1972 the majority of English and English-speaking Welsh Congregationalists joined with the Presbyterian Church of England to form the United Reformed Church. Has the Congregational understanding of the Church been preserved or lost within the united Church? If preserved, has it been fully appreciated in all its pastoral implications? If lost, does it matter? Could it be that (<u>pace</u> the continuing Congregationalists of the Federation [10] and the Evangelical Fellowship of Congregational Churches) the death of the <u>denomination</u> facilitated the flowering of the catholicity of the <u>ism</u>? On the pastoral side we shall enquire whether the idea of grounded sainthood is being consistently applied within the new Church.

In the attempt to answer these questions we shall find that 'a little spice of antiquity will not hurt us.'[11] On the contrary, it will be of the greatest benefit if it recalls us to our primary allegiance and promotes our present obedience. But quite apart from such a possible practical outcome, a spice of antiquity is indispensable if we would thoroughly understand the idea of which we treat. We must at the outset ask, 'What occasioned the separatist protest?' Positively, the protest originated in an insight into the way God calls his people to himself and gives them to each other; negatively, it was a reaction against unacceptable understandings and applications of church discipline.

During the Middle Ages the Church in the west increasingly assumed disciplinary rights over public institutions and private life. The bull <u>Unam Sanctam</u> (1302) of Boniface VIII declared that the Pope was head of both Church and State. In the wake of such harsh examples of discipline as the punishment by death of John Hus, Jerome of Prague, Wyclif and others; and of the widespread abuse of the system of indulgences, the Reformers and their followers turned to the newly-opened Bible to see what <u>it</u> said concerning ecclesiastical discipline. The Bible was regarded as authoritative in matters of faith, Christian living, and church order and practice. The pulpit assumed a new importance as the place from which biblical advice was promulgated and exhortations were made. If Luther did not bequeath a fully-elaborated system of discipline, Zwingli and, still more, Calvin did. They sought to restore to the State its proper rights, with the proviso that in churchly matters it should act as the representative of the Church.

Zwingli left the right of excommunication in the hands of the State, but he was concerned that the civil magistrates should be holy men of the Book. Their task was to make the preached principles a reality in the common life of the people. They did not possess their powers inherently and _ex officio_, as they might under an Erastian system, but were, in relation to ecclesiastical discipline, the representatives of the Church.[12] Calvin further developed this approach to the matter. With _Matt_. xviii 15 ff in mind he advised the private admonition of offenders where this was possible, and churchly deliberation in the case of more publicly-known offences. If the guilty would not repent, the State was to pass sentence, though excommunication remained the prerogative of the Church.[13]

The disciplinary practice of Zwingli and Calvin turned upon the viability as _Christian_ of the State-Church duality. But what if it were not Christian? In England ecclesiastical discipline became very much a matter of attempting to secure conformity - this for political as much as for religious reasons - hence the Acts of Uniformity of 1549, 1552 and 1559. But some considered that they were being required to conform to a godless State-Church wherein allegiance was given to Antichrist rather than to Christ. They could do no other than separate themselves from a false order with a view to establishing true and pure churches under the gospel. This was the motive which inspired the courage and prompted the actions of those who, however unwittingly, became the harbingers of modern congregationalism.

The Congregational Way gradually achieved clarity of definition. This occurred both as the founding fathers adumbrated the biblical basis of the way, and as the polity was distinguished from the episcopalian and presbyterian ecclesiologies which were in the field with it. An hierarchy of bishops appealed to the Congregationalists no more than did an hierarchy of Church courts, since both were held to weaken, and on occasion to obstruct, the direct rule of Christ, the head of the Church, over his gathered saints. Although we shall not provide detailed expositions of contemporary Anglican and Presbyterian polities,[14] it is important to remember that Congregationalism was pioneered in conscious opposition to them.

The position of Congregationalism as a distinct polity having been secured, there was, as early as 1690, the possibility of Congregational-Presbyterian union. But the projected Happy Union foundered, not least because many Congregationalists deplored that erosion of Calvinistic theology in which many Presbyterians acquiesced, and to which some of them positively contributed. It was to be a further two and a half centuries before moves resulting in union were to be instigated. By that time the Congregationalists had learned much more concerning the mutual relations of visibility, orderliness and catholicity within the general understanding of the Church as comprising saints. Nothing did more to foster this learning than the challenge to mission abroad and at home which was inherent in the Evangelical Revival of the second half of the eighteenth century. Initially in response to this challenge a more structured, corporately-churchly life gradually ensued, until that blend of independence and fellowship which county unions and the national Union had expressed, and of which Provincial Moderators became such an important symbol from 1919 onwards, found fulfilment in the Congregational Church in England and Wales; and thence in that episcope, in which both local churches and wider councils mutually share, which is so marked a feature of the polity of the United Reformed Church.

2. The Pre-history of Congregationalism

Congregationalists, no less than other Christians, have in the past sought to show that their polity was laid down by Christ himself. Paul's exhortation to the Corinthians that they 'separate themselves'[1] and, above all, Jesus's declaration that 'where two or three have met together in my name, I am there among them,'[2] were taken as clear indications that the true Church was separated - first, from the State (Robert Browne) and, later, to the Lord - and gathered under Christ. Attempts have from time to time been made to show that congregationalism with a small 'c' was never wholly absent from the Church's life, but it is not until the seventeenth century that, in a particular political environment, we find the beginnings of a formulated congregational ecclesiology. We find the seeds of Congregational practice in Richard Fitz's separatist congregation, and of Congregational theory in the writings of Robert Browne and his contemporaries. We detect a modification of the understanding of independence in the works of John Robinson; and the first harvest, in which charismatic zeal is tempered by Reformed orderliness, in the <u>Savoy Declaration of Faith and Order</u> (1658), and in the literary labours of its principal architect John Owen, and others. Common throughout is the idea that Christians are covenanted saints; though as

time passes there is an increasing willingness
to admit the idea that the saints are not only, or even necessarily, visibly gathered in
local churches. They may be distributed among
many visible churches as wheat among the
tares; in which event their true number and
identity is known to God alone. Common too is
the conviction that the political conclusions
reached have been given by the Spirit through
the Word. From this summary statement it
becomes clear both that, as befits a corporate
priesthood, Congregationalism owns no one
founding father; and that the _ism_ was from the
outset plastic. Congregationalism did not
erupt into the world fully grown.

Dr. H.M. Dexter surely goes too far in
saying of Richard Fitz's 1567 congregation
that its members 'seem to me like a company
driven by stress of storm to some uninhabited
land, and provisionally living there for a
time without any government, other than that
which the first law of self-preservation sup-
plied.'[3] Under storm of stress they undoubtedly were; makers of purely pragmatic re-
sponses they were not. The scanty evidence
they have left us reveals their main convic-
tions as to the marks of the Church: 'First
and formost, the Glorious word and Evangel
preached, not in bondage and subjection, but
freely, and purely. Secondly to have the Sacraments ministered purely, only and all together according to the institution and good
word of the Lord Jesus, without any tradition
or invention of man. And last of all to have,
not the filthy Canon law, but discipline only,
and all together agreeable to the same heavenly and almighty word of our good Lord, Jesus
Christ.'[4] Thus far we have, over Richard
Fitz's signature, an earnest of a number of
later Reformed statements concerning the nature

of the Church,[5] and to this extent Dexter was
correct in saying that 'These are good Congregational principles as far as they go, but
they scarcely more touch the question of pure
polity, than the pile driven deep below the
foundations of a building, suggests whether
that is to be Gothic, Grecian, or pure Yankee,
in its facade.'[6] A further stage is reached
when, in what appears to be their local covenant the members of Fitz's congregation justify their separatism:

> Being thoroughly persuaded in my con-
> science, by the working and by the word
> of the almighty, that these relics of
> Antichrist be abominable before the Lord
> our God.
>
> And also for that by the power and
> mercy, strength and goodness of the Lord
> my God only, I am escaped from the
> filthiness and pollution of these de-
> testable traditons, through the know-
> ledge of our Lord and saviour Jesus
> Christ:
>
> And last of all, inasmuch as by the
> working also of the Lord Jesus his holy
> spirit, I have joined in prayer, and
> hearing God's word, with those that have
> not yielded to this idolatrous trash,
> notwithstanding the danger for not com-
> ing to my parish church.&c,
>
> Therefore I come not back again to
> the preachings.&c, of them that have re-
> ceived these marks of the Romish beast.
>
> 1. Because of God's commandment to go
> forward to perfection...Also to avoid
> them...
>
> 2. Because they are abominations before
> the Lord our God...
>
> 3. I will not beautify with my presence

those filthy rags, which bring the heavenly word of the eternal our Lord God,
into bondage, subjection, and slavery.

4. Because I would not communicate with
other men's sins...Touch no unclean
thing.&c.

5. They give offences, both the preacher
and the hearers...

6. They glad and strengthen the Papists
in their error, and grieve the godly...

7. They do persecute our saviour Jesus
Christ in his members...Also they reject
and despise our Lord and saviour Jesus
Christ...Moreover those labourers, whom
at the prayer of the faithful, the Lord
hath sent forth into his harvest they
refuse, and also reject...

8. These Popish garments &c, are now
become very Idols indeed, because they
are exalted above the word of the almighty.

9. I come not to them because they
should be ashamed, and so leave their
Idolatrous garments,&c...If any man obey
not our sayings, note him.&c. God give
us strength still to strive in suffering
under the cross, that the blessed word
of our God may only rule, and have the
highest place, to cast down strongholds,
to destroy or overthrow policies or
imaginations, and every high thing that
is exalted against the knowledge of God,
and to bring into captivity or subjection, every thought to the obedience of
Christ. &c...that the name and word of
the eternal our Lord God, may be exalted
or magnified above all things...[7]

The sincerity and courage of the members of
Fitz's 'Privy Church' is unquestionable, but

we are still far from the pneumatic ethos
which was to mark the position of John
Robinson and Henry Barrow, who could <u>deny</u> that
preaching and sacraments are necessary marks
of the church,[8] and whose motive seems to have
been spiritual and moral before it was
ecclesiological.[9] It would not, of course,
have occurred to these separatists that the
dominical sacraments should <u>not</u> be observed;
that baptism did not signify entry into the
covenant; or that the Lord's Supper was an
optional extra in church life. The point rather was - and none put it more regularly, or
more stridently, than Barrow - that a true
church only could truly observe the sacraments; and that the performance of rites and
ceremonies by an unworthy church was nothing
more than a hypocritical sham.

Richard Fitz and his fellow-sufferers were
but the harbingers of Congregational <u>theory,</u>
and for the first full literary treatment of
that we must turn to Robert Browne (c.1550-
1633). But although theory begins now to come
into its own, we must not be too coldly cere-
bral about it. Browne was no professional
theory-monger. Far from it; it has been well
said that he 'perceived, as by sudden illumi-
nation, the glorious liberty of the children
of God as expressed in the voluntary fellow-
ships and charismatic ministries of the New
Testament.'[10] Moreover others, if not Browne
himself, were prepared to die for the vision
they had seen.[11]

Browne was impelled into separatism in
1576, and constituted his society in Norwich
in 1581. He was decidedly <u>not</u> an advocate of
the complete separation of Church from state.
The Prince had his rights and responsibilities
- even to the extent of wielding the sword in
the interests of law and order;[12] but Browne

would have echoed the sentiments of a member
of a separatist church in London (c.1567) who
said concerning the Queen that 'Our bodies,
goods, and lives be at her commandment, and
she shall have them as of true subjects. But
the soul of man for religion is bound to none
but unto God and His Holy Word.'[13] For their
part, the saints had duties; and if a false
Church should render impossible the fulfilment
of those duties, then separation from that
Church became itself a duty. Browne was clear
that the mere fact of residence within a parish did not make a person a Christian, and
from the New Testament he 'deduced' the doctrine that 'the Kingdom of God Was not to be
begun by whole parishes, but rather of the
worthiest, Were they never so few.'[14] Consistently with this he holds that Christians
are those who 'by a willing Covenant made with
our God...are under the government of God and
Christ, and thereby do lead a godly and christian life.'[15] Such comprise the Church: 'The
Church planted or gathered, is a company or
number of Christians or believers, which by a
willing covenant made with their God, are
under the government of Christ, and keep his
laws in one holy communion...'[16] He elsewhere
reinforced the voluntariness of church membership when he declared that 'the Lord's people is of the willing sort.'[17] The government
of the Church is Christ's alone; it is 'the
Lordship of Christ in the communion of his
offices: whereby his people obey to his will,
and have mutual use of their graces and
callings, to further their godliness and
welfare.'[18]

Browne was not an out and out individualist. He has a place for synods, albeit of an
advisory kind: and, what is more, synods are
to be gatherings of entire local churches, and

not only of representatives therefrom: 'A Synod is a Joining or partaking of the authority of many Churches met together in peace, for redress, and deciding of matters, which cannot well be otherwise taken up.'[19] As A.M. Fairbairn was much later to insist, 'There is nothing less true than that Brownism regarded any church member as a private person, or a church as a private association.'[20] To the separatist 'The kingdom of God was a kingdom of the godly; the Church of Christ was a society of Christian men;'[21] and all else - the election of officers, the disciplining of the flock - followed from that principle. If to the hostile Thomas Nash the independents seemed to be 'a company of malcontents, unworthy to breathe on the earth,'[22] to themselves, at their least arrogant, they were purchased, undeserving saints. They were also an equal body of kings and priests: 'every one of the church is made a King, a Priest, and a Prophet under Christ, to uphold and further the Kingdom of God, and to break and destroy the kingdom of Antichrist, and Satan.'[23] Such teaching as this shaped the separatist view of the ministry.

It remains only to note the diverse attitudes, ranging from veneration, through ambivalence, to abhorrence, adopted by Browne's successors to Browne himself. Thus, whereas later writers such as Thomas Wall[24] advocated the extreme separatism of Browne, Barrowe and the early Robinson, Ainsworth and Johnson, themselves suspicious of over-much democracy and, perhaps, dismayed by Browne's eventual return to the Church of England (1586), spoke in 1604 of their Amsterdam congregation as comprising 'such true Christians, as are commonly (but unjustly) called Brownists.'[25] As for those who made their way to New England:

though Puritans, they were by no means separatists; and we can hardly be surprised if those
who, at great cost, sought to build a godly
Establishment in a new land should be inclined
to disown Browne, take to themselves the name
'Congregational,' and employ 'Brownist' as a
term of abuse. Champlin Burrage's verdict is
just: 'Robert Browne, at an early stage of his
career, may be truly called a pioneer of what
today is known as Congregationalism, but a
long period of evolution intervenes between
him and present-day Congregationalists and
Independents. His connection with the first
Independents (or first Congregationalists) in
likewise rather indirect.'[26]

Henry Barrow (c.1550-93) was more of an
icoloclast than Browne. Like the early
Robinson, he would have eradicated all false
churches. In a typical passage his zeal, and
his justification of separation from a corrupt
Establishment, emerge:

> We must not (say they) forsake the
> church, nor the ordinance of God, for
> the sins of any, either minister or peo-
> ple: for a godly conscience is not hurt
> with the sins of another, neither the
> ministry or sacraments therewith de-
> filed. If they mean here by the church,
> the assembly and communion of God's
> faithful obedient servants... I grant
> that the church, ministry, and ordi-
> nances of Christ, are not to be left, or
> thought the worse of for the sin of
> men... But if they mean (as all their
> reasoning imports) by the church and
> ordinances of God, such wicked rebel-
> lious assemblies, as reject the word of
> God, with an high hand break his law,
> despise admonition, hate to be reformed,
> receive and retain the open unworthy,

wicked, impenitent to their sacraments, etc., I then deny these assemblies to be the true churches of Christ; seeing they have broken the covenant...As also I deny their sacraments to be the ordinances of God...[27]

In his fourth examination by the Council on 18th March 1588/9[28] Barrow was even more specific:

Lord Treasurer.	Why will you not go to church?
Barrow.	My whole desire is to come to the church of God.
Lord Treasurer.	Thou art a fantastical fellow I see, but why not to our churches?
Barrow.	My lord, the causes are great and many; it were too long to shew them in particular: but briefly, my lord, I cannot come to your church 1.Because all the profane and wicked of the land are received into the body of your church. 2.You have a false and antichristian ministry set over your church. 3.Neither worship you God aright, but after an idolatrous and superstitious manner. 4.And your church is not governed by Christ's Testament (by the word

of God), but by the Romish courts and canons.[29]

It is noteworthy that the Americans H.M. Dexter and Williston Walker find a divergence between the thought of Browne and that of Barrow. The former, they argue, maintained the equality of the membership, whereas the latter's system accommodated elders conceived as a ruling oligarchy.[30] When this view is measured by Barrow's own words it is difficult to sustain it, and we may suspect that the distinguished representatives of the more traditionally consistorial Congregationalism of America found what they sought in Barrow. 'Elders,' said Barrow, 'are appointed to see the government and order of Christ observed, not to take it all into their hands;'[31] and of church officers in general he wrote, 'I never thought that the practise of Christ's government belonged only to these officers; I rather thought it had been their duty and office to have seen this government faithfully and orderly practised by all the members of the church.'[32]

No one makes more of what we have called the earthed nature of Congregational sainthood than Barrow. On one occasion Lancelot Andrewes visited Barrow in prison, and during the course of conversation he said, 'The solitary and contemplative life I hold the most blessed life. It is the life I would choose.' If this was a pastoral ploy designed to cheer an incarcerated brother (as well as a personal conviction - we impute no hypocrisy to Andrewes) it did not work. Barrow replied, 'You speak philosophically, but not Christianly. So sweet is the harmony of God's grace unto me in the congregation, and the conversation of the saints at all times, as I think myself as a sparrow on the housetop when I am exiled from them.'[33]

The position of John Greenwood (d.1593) follows closely that of his fellow prisoner and martyr, Barrow. In his defense before the Lord Chief Justices on 24th March 1588/9, in answer to the question,'Do you not hold a parish the church?' he replied,'If all the people were faithful, having God's law and ordinances practised amongst them, I do.' The interrogation proceeded thus:

> Question: Then you hold that the parish do not make it a church?
>
> Answer: No, but the profession which the people make.
>
> Question: Do you hold that the church ought to be governed by a presbytery?
>
> Answer: Yea, every congregation of Christ ought to be governed by that presbytery which Christ hath appointed.
>
> Question: What are those officers?
>
> Answer: Pastor, teacher, elder,etc...
>
> Question: May this people and presbytery reform such things as be a-miss, without the prince?
>
> Answer: They ought to practice God's laws, and correct vice by the censure of the word.
>
> Question: What if the prince forbid them?
>
> Answer: They must do that which God commandeth, nevertheless.[34]

In The True Church and the False Church (1588), a work whose writing Barrow may have shared with Greenwood, but with which the latter was in full sympathy, the case is reaffirmed:

> The true planted and rightly established
> church of Christ is a company of faith-
> ful people; separated from the unbeliev-
> ers and heathen of the land; gathered in
> the name of Christ, whom they truly wor-
> ship, and readily obey as their only
> king, priest, and prophet; joined to-
> gether as members of one body; ordered
> and governed by such officers and laws
> as Christ in his last will and testament
> hath thereunto ordained; all and each
> one of them standing in and for their
> christian liberty to practise whatsoever
> God hath commanded and revealed unto
> them in his holy word within the limits
> of their callings, executing the Lord's
> judgments against all transgression and
> disobedience which ariseth among them,
> and cutting it off accordingly by the
> power which their Lord and King, Christ
> Jesus, hath committed unto them.[35]

The importance of John Robinson (c.1575-
1625) cannot be over-estimated if we would
gauge the development of Congregationalism in
the early years of the seventeenth century. An
exile though not himself a Pilgrim, he was
pastor to those who became the Pilgrim Fathers, and was undoubtedly possessed of a pilgrim mind: and this not least concerning ecclesiological matters. Indeed, Dexter argued
that Robinson's famous declaration to the de-
parting Pilgrims that 'The Lord hath yet more
light and truth to break forth out of his holy
Word' was made with reference to the ordering
of church life.'[36] Certainly the covenant of
the church at Scrooby, whose pastor Robinson
had been, contained the pledge of the members
'To walk together in all God's ways, made
known, or to be made known to them.' One thing

would never change, however: the Church would
always comprise the saints, and at its best
the fellowship of the local church could be
likened only to heaven: 'If ever I saw the
beauty of Zion, and the glory of the Lord
filling His tabernacle, it hath been in the
manifestation of the diverse graces of God in
the Church, in that heavenly harmony and
comely order wherin, by the grace of God, we
are set and walk.'[37]

The religion of the State-Church was, by
contrast, grievously impoverished. At first
Robinson was quite intolerant: 'the whole communion in the Church of England, is so pol-
luted, with profane and scandalous persons, as
that even in this respect alone, were there
none other, there were just cause of separation from it.'[38] Four years later Robinson is
prepared to concede that in practice a distinction must be drawn between the true church
and the visible church.[39] Later still he declares that the catholic Church is invisi-
ble;[40] and when he publishes his A Treatise on
the Lawfulness of Hearing Ministers in the
Church of England (1634, but written earlier),
we find him at his most eirenic. He informs us
that God can bless the truths taught even by
an unlawful officer; he reminds us that even
if the Anglican system is to be deplored, the
fact remains that its officers do not get
their gospel from the bishops, but from God;
and he urges mutual charity and compassion
within the Church.[41]

Robinson's positive view of church order
may be summarized as follows: 'only saints,
that is , a people forsaking all known sin of
which they may be convinced, doing all the
known will of God, increasing and abiding ever
therein, are the only matter of the visible
church...The power of Christ...belongeth to

the whole church, yea to every one of them,
and not [only?] to the principle members
thereof...A company, consisting though but of
two or three...gathered into the name of
Christ by a covenant made to walk in all the
ways of God known unto them is a church...So
far are the officers from being the formal
cause of the church...they are, in truth, no
absolutely necessary appurtenance unto it...
And the reason is, because the church is essentially in the saints, as the matter, subject, formed by the covenant, unto which the
officers are but adjuncts, not making for the
being, but for the well-being of the church,
and furtherance of her faith, by their service...The Lord Jesus is the king of his church
alone, upon whose shoulders the government is,
and unto whom all power is given in heaven and
earth; yet hath he not received this power for
himself alone, but doth communicate the same
with his church, as the husband with the
wife...And in this holy fellowship, by virtue
of this plenteous anointment, every one is
made a king, priest, and prophet, not only to
himself but to every other, yea to the
whole...There is not the meanest member of the
body but hath received his drop or dram of
this anointing... [Nevertheless some] are to
be set over the rest [but their office is] not
kingly but ministerial. [This is] according to
the testament of Christ [and is] not only for
comeliness and order...No particular church
under the New Testament, ought to consist of
more members than can meet together in one
place.'[42] The idea that church order was something more than a matter of expediency is one
which certain nineteenth-century Congregationalists would have found hard to stomach, as we
shall see.

Towards the end of his life Robinson could

say that he was in 'all Christian fellowship'
with true Christians everywhere,[43] and he concluded his <u>Just and Necessary Apology</u> (1619,
Latin;1625) with a characteristic prayer: 'Towards thee, O Lord, are our eyes; confirm our
hearts, and bend thine ear, and suffer not our
feet to slip, or our face to be ashamed, O
thou just and most merciful God. To him
through Christ be praise, for ever, in the
church of saints; and to thee, loving and
Christian reader, grace, peace, and eternal
happiness. Amen.'[44]

Influenced by, and a moderating influence
upon, Robinson was Henry Jacob (1563?-1624),
to whom Neal accorded the honour (<u>pace</u> earlier
separatist congregations) of gathering the
first Congregational church in England (1616):

> Some time after he returned to England,
> and having imparted his design of
> setting up a separate congregation, like
> those in Holland, to the most learned
> puritans of those times, it was not con-
> demned as unlawful, considering there
> was no prospect of a national reforma-
> tion. Mr. Jacob therefore having sum-
> moned several of his friends together,
> and having obtained their consent to
> unite in church-fellowship, for enjoying
> the ordinances of Christ in the purest
> manner, they laid the foundation of the
> first Independent, or congregational
> church in England, after the following
> manner. Having observed a day of solemn
> fasting and prayer for a blessing upon
> their undertaking, towards the close of
> the solemnity each of them made open
> confession of their faith in our Lord
> Jesus Christ; and then standing together
> they joined hands, and solemnly cove-

nanted with each other in the presence
of Almighty God, to walk together in all
God's ways and ordinances, according as
he had already revealed, or should
further make known to them. Mr. Jacob
was then chosen pastor by the suffrage
of the brotherhood, and others were appointed to the office of deacons, with
fasting and prayer and imposition of
hands.[45]

That Jacob's ecclesiological views were
largely formed ten years before he founded his
church is clear from his catechism of 1604/5:

Question: What is a true Visible or Ministerial Church of Christ?
Answer: A True Visible or Ministerial
Church of Christ is a particular Congregation being a
spiritual perfect Corporation
of Believers, and having power
in itself immediately from
Christ to administer all Religious means of faith to the
members thereof.
Question: How is a Visible Church constituted and gathered?
Answer: By a free mutual consent of
Believers joining and covenanting to live as Members of
a holy Society together in all
religious and virtuous duties
as Christ and his Apostles did
institute and practise in the
Gospel. By such a free mutual
consent also all Civil perfect Corporations did first
begin.[46]

The political unacceptability to many of
such a church order prompted Jacob to write
his <u>A Confession and Protestation of the Faith
of Certaine Christians in England</u> (1616). The
inordinately long title given to this pamphlet
contains the explanation that the work is
'Published for the clearing of the said
Christians from the slander of Schism, and
Novelty, and also of Separation, and unduti-
fulness to the Magistrate, which their rash
Adversaries do falsely cast upon them. Also an
humble Petition to the King's Majesty for Toleration therein.'

In the evidence thus far given we have
variations upon the theme of the 1589 Confession, <u>A True Description out of the Word of
God of the Visible Church</u>.[47] Such a church
comprises the elect of God, and it is properly
ordered. But, above all, its members are
saints. R.W. Dale drew out the crucial ecclesiological point which is the foundation of
all the views we have so far considered: 'Congregationalism was a serious attempt to rec-
ognize in the organization of the Church the
infinite difference between those who are in
Christ and those who are not, between the
living and the dead, the saved and the lost.
The great prerogatives which it attributed to
the Church assumed that the Church consisted
of persons who had received the life of
Christ. The independence of every separate
community of the faithful was an immediate
corollary from these prerogatives.'[48]

Dr. Alexander Mackennal set the same point
in its historical context thus:

> As the existence of spiritual life in
> those who come together, a new birth
> from above, is the one indispensable
> foundation of a Congregational church,

it is interesting to notice that it was
the revival of spiritual life which
first led to the revival of the Congregational system among the early English
Separatists. The ecclesiastical idea did
not come first, but the spiritual. The
breath of God breathed upon the souls of
men, and, weary of priestly superstition
and unreality, they resolved at all
hazards to get at the fountains of life
for themselves. In doing this they went
back behind all the piled-up traditions
of centuries of corruption and asked -
What saith the Lord? The Scriptures were
once more lifted into the place of authority in Church life, and with the revival of Apostolic teaching came the revival of Apostolic practice. The Eliza-
bethan congregationalists certainly never dreamt for a moment that they had
invented anything new. They believed
themselves to be simply reverting to the
true antiquity.[49]

Those whom we have considered in this chapter belonged to companies of freely covenanted
saints, conscious that they have been called
by grace to be the people of a God who had
made himself supremely known in Christ and
who, in the scriptures, had provided all needful guidance for doctrine and life. They made
no purely pedestrian plea against state interference in religion; it would be anachronistic
to represent them as being primarily concerned
with the rights of the individual. On the contrary, 'so far as the individual was affected
they laid more stress on his duties and responsibilities than on his rights.'[50] The
rights they were concerned about were God's.
They desired to give him alone the glory - and

this on the basis of a view of scripture according to which 'the New Testament contained
a revelation of infinite glory and of infinite
terror. Its menaces were as real as its pro-
mises.'[51]

3. Classical Congregationalism, 1640-1690

In investigating the classical Congregational doctrine of the Church we must take due account of the New World, and that for three reasons. First, unlike the Scrooby-Leyden Pilgrims who established the Plymouth colony in 1620, the later waves of Puritan exiles - beginning with John Endecott's party which landed at Salem, Massachusetts in 1628 - were not separatists in temperament. Or, at least, their separatism was very much more a matter of separation from the world than from a particular, corrupt, State-Church. As good Puritans they were not opposed to establishments as such. On the contrary, their intention was to inaugurate a godly commonwealth in their new home. The ecclesiological foundations upon which they built, derived as they were from the New Testament, were largely identical with those of Plymouth. Secondly, while owning the full the rights, privileges and duties of the local church, they were much more positive than the earlier separatists in their advocacy of what they came to call 'consociation.' Certainly such zealous individualists as Cromwell's chaplains John Saltmarsh and William Dell would have had little patience with consociation. Thirdly, it was when he set out to refute John Cotton's <u>The Keyes of the Kingdom</u> (1644) that John Owen became a convert to Congregationalism. A New World apology for

Congregationalism could hardly have had a more
significant result.

We shall briefly review a representative
selection of writings, local church covenants,
and more formal confessions of faith, with a
view to tracing the development of the Congregational idea of the Church, and detecting the
variations played upon the main theme. Since
the matters with which we are concerned are
inextricably interwoven we shall not artifi-
cially separate out what individual writers
said first on sainthood, then on independence,
then on fellowship. Rather, we shall procede
chronologically within each category of material, observing differences of emphasis, but
also endeavouring to take the full force of
what was by now an increasingly cogently ar-
ticulated ecclesiology, propounded in conscious opposition to both episcopalianism and
presbyterianism.

John Cotton (d.1652), who had been Vicar of
Boston, Lincolnshire for twenty-one years, em-
igrated to America in 1633, and became pastor
of the Congregational church at Trimountain
(subsequently Boston).[1] In the very next year
there appeared his <u>Questions and Answers upon
Church Government</u>, the first of a number of
Congregational apologies to come from his pen.
He follows the general direction taken by
Robinson, though over the vexed question of
ruling elders, which had exercised the exiles
in Middelburg, Amsterdam and Leyden, he upheld
their status and saw them as responsible for
the business of the local church. (We shall
have more to say concerning ruling elders when
we come to the formal declarations of faith).

Church practice in New England attracted
increasing attention in England, and from 1637
onwards a series of questions was addressed to
the expatriates by the English Presbyterians.

Richard Mather's reply was entitled Church-
Government and Church-Covenant Discussed
(1643). Such affirmations as the following
greatly strengthened the hand of those Independents who were in the same year to participate in the Westminster Assembly: 'When a
Visible Church is to be erected, planted, or
constituted, by the Appointment of Christ, it
is necessary that the matter of it in regard
of quality, should be Saints by calling, Visible Christians and Believers...And in respect
of Quantity no more in number in the days of
the New Testament, but so many as may meet in
one Congregation...'[2]

The Westminster Assembly included among its
largely Presbyterian number the five Independent brethren, Thomas Goodwin, Philip Nye,
Sidrach Simpson, Jeremiah Burroughes and
William Bridge. They submitted An Apologeticall Narration to Parliament in which they
adumbrated their distinctive position. It was
a position reached after a deliberate and
painstaking search of the scriptures. They set
themselves 'to search out what were the first
Apostolic directions, pattern and examples of
those Primitive Churches recorded in the New
Testament...In this enquiry we looked upon the
Word of Christ as impartially, and unpreju-
dicedly, as men of flesh and blood are like to
do... Our situation leaving us as freely to be
guided by that light and touch God's Spirit
should by the Word vouchsafe to our con-
sciences...'[3]

On the question of church membership the
signatories declare that 'the Rules which we
gave up our judgments unto, to judge those we
received in amongst us by, were of that lati-
tude as would take in any member of Christ...
We took measure of no man's holiness by his
own opinion, whether concurring with us, or

adverse unto us.'[4] Cautious oncerning the powers of Presbyterian assemblies, they contend
that 'the first Churches planted by the Apostles, were ordinarily of no more in one city
at first than might make up one entire congregation,[5] ruled by their own Elders, that also
preached to them...We could not therefore but
judge it a safe and an allowed way to retain
the government of our several congregations
for the matter of discipline within themselves, to be exercised by their own Elders...
yet not claiming to ourselves an <u>independent
power</u> in every congregation, to give account
or be subject to none others, but only a full
and entire power complete within ourselves,
until we should be challenged to err
grossly.' When such a thing happened it was
quite in order that the offending church
should undergo 'the most full and open trial
by other neighbouring Churches,' and that fellowship should be withheld from such a church
until evidence of repentance was provided.[6]

The five Independents do not see themselves
as fostering schism within the Reformed communion by proclaiming that the Calvinistic
churches 'do stand in need of a further reformation.'[7] They do not see themselves as sedi-
tious isolationists, and they vehemently disown 'That proud and insolent title of Independency.'[8] Rather, in exile and again now
they 'do here publicly profess, we believe the
truth to lie and consist in a <u>middle way</u> be-
tweixt that which is falsely charged on us,
<u>Brownism</u>; and that which is the contention of
these times, the <u>authoritative Presbyterial
Government</u> in all the subordinations and proceedings of it.'[9] As Thomas Goodwin later
wrote, 'Though particular churches are not
subject to the jurisdiction of synods, yet
they are not wholly independent, but there is

communion which they ought to hold with one another.'[10] The Independent divines thus emphasise the necessity of a properly elected eldership, and they have a place for the wider fellowship of churches. They may perhaps be placed between the early Robinson and Presbyterianism.

That Jeremiah Burroughes was in complete agreement with his Independent colleagues is clear from his replies to Thomas Edwards's virulent _Antiapologia_ (1644) and _Gangraena_ (1646). In his _Vindication_ (1644) and _Irenicum_ (1646)[11] Burroughes makes clear the proper, advisory and disciplinary function of synods.

The influence of Cotton's _The Keyes of the Kingdom_ cannot be overestimated. It was commended to the public by Thomas Goodwin and Philip Nye, and its moderation was such that the Scottish Presbyterian, Samuel Rutherford, thought it provided a basis for Presbyterian-Independent union negotiations. The one thing needful, he thought, was that the Independents should give 'a little more power to Synods.'[12] Cotton argues that the local church has the power to elect its officers, to send out evangelists, and to exercise discipline. Furthermore, 'By way of Consultation, one church hath liberty of communication with another to require their judgments and counsel, touching any person or cause, wherewith they may be better acquainted than themselves.'[13] The elders are to rule, and their duties include preaching, the examination of candidates for church membership, the ordaining of officers, and the conduct of the business of the church. Rightly ordered synods are an ordinance of Christ, and consociation is eminently desirable, for 'Though the Church of a particular Congregation, consisting of Elders and Brethren, and walking with a right foot in

the truth and peace of the Gospel, be the
first subject of all Church-power needful to
be exercised within itself; and consequently
be independent from any other Church of Synod
in the use of it; yet it is a safe, and whole-
some, and holy Ordinance of Christ, for such
particular Churches to join together in holy
Covenant or communion, and consolation amongst
themselves, to administer all their Church
affairs (which are of weighty, and difficult
and common concernment) not without common
consultation and consent of other Churches
about them.'[14]

Much the same ground was taken by John Cook
in his apology for the Independents which appeared in 1647. An Independent, he writes,
'holds a subordination of Officers in the same
Church, but an equality in several Congregations; which as sisters depend not upon one
another, but are helpful as one hand to another.'[15] Perhaps with such co-operative Presbyterians as Rutherford in mind, Cook avers that
the Independent 'counts every godly Presbyterian to be his dear brother, but not to be
preferred before the truth.'[16] In the same
year William Bartlett of Wapping published
his Ἰχνογραφία, or a Model of the Primitive
Congregational Way, in which he argued that
there are good and bad forms of separation. It
is good to be separated from sin, false worship, and the like; it is bad to be separated
from Christ and to the Devil. Needless to say,
the Congregationalists are worthy separatists,
but his account of their ecclesiology, of
which the following quotation is the kernel,
is not one which requires him positively to
advocate consociation:

> There is under the New Testament a
> sacred visible Church-state, order and

> polity, instituted and appointed by Jesus Christ, and him only, to the observation of which, Believers are everywhere bound, willingly to submit and subject themselves...This visible Church-state is a free society of visible Saints, embodied or knit together, by a voluntary consent, in holy fellowship, to worship God according to his word, consisting of one ordinary congregation, with power of government in itself...The godly are bound everywhere, to gather themselves into such a Church-state if they are of a competent number, or to join themselves to such Churches as are already gathered.[17]

Since the national Church contains both wheat and tares it cannot, says Bartlett, be a true Church. At this point Burroughes is invoked: 'That we may call the Church in England a National Church because of the many Saints in it, who are the body of Christ, I deny not...but that it is by the institution of Christ formed into one political Church, as the Nation of the Jews was, this is no Independency to deny. Where are any particular men standing Church Officers to the whole Nation by divine institution? What National worship hath Christ instituted? Doth our birth in the Nation make us members of the Church?'[18] To all of these questions Bartlett, like Burroughes before him, expected resoundingly negative replies.

Before the 1640s were out a further important work emanated from America: A Survey of the Summe of Church Discipline, Wherein the Way of the Churches of New England is warranted out of the Word (1648), by Thomas Hooker, sometime pastor at Harford, Connecticut.

Christ is the Head of the Church, we are told,
and the Church is his mystical body: 'The mystical Body is the Church of true Believers,
who being effectually called by his word and
spirit, by faith yielding to the call, are
spiritually united unto Christ, from whom, as
from a head, all spiritual life and motion is
communicated on his part, and received on
theirs...Visible Saints only are fit Matter
appointed by God to make up a visible Church
of Christ...Mutual covenanting and confeder-
ating of the Saints in the fellowship of the
faith according to the order of the Gospel, is
that which gives constitution and being to a
visible Church.'[19] Such a covenanted body has
the duty and privilege of electing officers;[20]
and 'Ordination is an approbation of the Officer, and solemn settling and confirmation of
him in his Office, by Prayer and the laying on
of hands.'[21]

In Part Two of his work Hooker attempts to
penetrate the haze still surrounding the term
'Independency.' It can imply absolute suprema-
cy (i.e. contra subordination), or sufficiency
in its kind for the attainment of its end (i.e
contra imperfection). Since consociation is
practised, the local church may be said to be
independent in the second sense.[22] Like others
writing from America Hooker had no qualms concerning consociation: it is 'not only lawful,
but very useful also.'[23] Synods may be provincial, national or even ecumenical. Their
power, which is not limitless, is held under
Christ.

We need give no further examples of Congregational ecclesiology as expounded by the
fathers in the first flush of pamphleteering.
Instead, we shall take one sounding from a
quarter of a century on , and then turn to the
writings of two men who sum up so much of Con-

gregational theory: Isaac Chauncy and John Owen.

Stephen Ford's A Gospel-Church, or God's Holy Temple Opened (1675) has, on the one hand, a more technically theological flavour than some of the works we have noted so far; and on the other hand there is not the somewhat strident defence of Independency that was common in earlier years. It is as if the Congregational polity had by now sufficiently differentiated itself from other polities; that the case for separation had been made; and all that was required was the more reflective reiteration of the theme. Moreover, the cadences of federal Calvinism begin to come through: indeed Ford's book begins with a strong declaration that the Church is founded upon the covenant of grace. Church members are quick and enlivened persons; they are God's regenerated workmanship; they have been bought with the blood of Christ; they are built on Christ and on the covenant of grace; they are fellow-citizens with the saints and of the household of God. There then follows the most balanced concise statement of both the Godward and manward factors leading to church membership that we have seen:

> A true Instituted Gospel-Church is, a
> Society of Congregation of persons
> called out of the world, or their state
> of death, blindness and unbelief, by the
> Word and Spirit of Christ; to the know-
> ledge of Christ and his will, and unto
> the Obedience of faith: or, A company of
> Believers united together in a holy
> Band, by special and voluntary agree-
> ment; who by the grace and power of
> Christ in their hearts under the convic-
> tion of their duty, do give themselves

up to the Lord, and to one another by
the will of God; and live and walk together as Saints, in love, peace, and in
the constant celebration and practice of
all the Law and worship of Christ; and
in the observation of all his Gospel-
Ordinances, in Obedience to his Holy
Will, for his glory and their Spiritual
profit.[24]

Isaac Chauncy's _The Divine Institution_
(1697) may be taken as summing up the generally received position at the end of the seventeenth century:

An artificial Building is not a Church;
for the Apostle Paul wrote his Epistles
to Churches, which could not be Dead-
walls, but to a People...It is not God's
Church which Man builds...God never gave
Commission to the Pope, Ecclesiastical
or Civil Powers to institute Churches;
and as the Church is of God, so the
whole form and fashion is of God's
teaching only...Every Church of Christ
is made of select Persons, and separated
from the World, either by Effectual
Calling, and thereby become Members of
the Mystical Body of Christ, or by a
visible Profession and Confederation,
and thereby become Members of the visible particular Churches...The end of
Church-Union is Communion, which is with
Christ the Head and one another...The
Catholic Church is the Mystical Body of
Christ made up of all saved ones, Mili-
tant and Triumphant, united together in
one Spirit, for communion therein accordingly...A Visible Church is a Particular Assembly of Professing Believers,

> visibly embodied in Christ, for a stated
> and holy Communion in one place, with
> God and one another, in all instituted
> Ordinances, appertaining to themselves
> and their immediate need, for God's Glo-
> ry in Christ, and their mutual Edifica-
> tion...Either a Congregational Church is
> of Divine Institution, or else God hath
> no instituted Church; for there is no
> other visible Church of God's Institu-
> tion spoken of in Scripture...A Visible
> Church is a spiritual Body of Believers,
> with their immediate Seed, separate from
> the World, and given up unto Christ and
> one another in a Public Covenant...We
> may benefit by each others Gifts and
> Graces...There is Communion in counsel
> and advice.[25]

Here we see clearly stated the belief that
Congregationalism is not simply one among many
church orders which may be derived from the
Bible: it is the only one which may be so derived. This view was later to be challenged,
not least by Congregationalists themselves. We
see too the implied counter to the Baptists,
namely that believers _and their immediate seed_
together comprise the Church. The discussion
of this view is perennial.

Supreme among the English Congregational
apologists was John Owen (1616-83), though it
cannot be said that he was in all respects
typical of his Congregational fellows. True,
as regards the 'autonomy-fellowship' polarity
within Congregationalism he traversed what he
called 'the valley (I had almost said the pit)
of _democratical confusion_ and the precipitous
rock of _hierarchy tyranny_;'[26] but _temperamen-_
tally his sympathies were more with the Reformed concern for order than with the

Anabaptist openness to the Spirit. Even this judgment must, however, be tempered by the recognition that Owen wrote a full-scale _Pneumatologia: Or a Discourse Concerning the Holy Spirit_ (1674); and it is clear from his Discourses Concerning the Holy Spirit (1693) that he did not deny the importance for ministry of the charismatic. Freedom within order was his objective.

Owen was by no means an iconoclastic separatist. While separation must be 'from the world and men of the world, with all ways of false worship...causeless separation from established Churches...is no small sin.'[27] It is not without significance that he attributed his conversion from Presbyterianism to Congregationalism to a reading of Cotton's _Keyes,_ which he had set out to refute.[28] Not surprisingly consociation, and the place of properly-regarded synods weighed heavily with him. Even so, Daniel Cawdry correctly observed that Owen did not, like the New Englanders, make particular churches a species of the universal Church.[29] To Owen the catholic Church comprises all the saints together, rather than the sum of all particular congregations.[30] The Church catholic is logically prior to the church local. Despite his divergence from other Congregational writers on certain points, Owen had come to be utterly convinced that 'Congregational Churches alone suited unto the ends of Christ in the Institution of his church;' and 'No other church-state of divine institution.'[31]

Owen's ecclesiological ideas find their classical expression in his posthumously published _The True Nature of a Gospel Church and Its Government_. He is quite clear that a local church is a disciplined fellowship of the regenerate, and he is more definite than Barrow and Robinson on the point that 'Of this regeneration baptism is the symbol, the sign, the expression and representation.'[32] We must not, of course, mistake the sign for the substance - 'God alone is judge concerning this regeneration, as unto its <u>internal, real principle and state</u> in the souls of men.'[33] From the human side, 'The way or means whereby such persons as are described in the foregoing chapter may become a church, or enter into a church-state, is by <u>mutual confederation</u> or solemn agreement for the performance of all the duties which the Lord Christ hath prescribed unto his disciples in such churches, and in order to the exercise of the power wherewith they are entrusted according unto the rule of the word.'[34]

The church's primary allegiance is to Christ, its Head: 'The rule of the church is, in general, <u>the exercise of the power or authority of Jesus Christ, given unto it, according to the laws and directions</u> prescribed <u>by himself, unto its edification.</u>'[35] Christ is the supreme authority in his Church; the power of men is 'ministerial only.' Where there are two or three believers '<u>right or power</u> is granted unto them actually to meet together in the name of Christ for their mutual edification.'[36] But - and this theme will be sounded loudly in succeeding ages by those Congregationalists who emphasize church order - not <u>any</u> two or three comprise a church. Owen cannot conceive of a church devoid of properly appointed officers.[37] The duties of elders and deacons are discussed at length; ecclesiastical discipline is advocated; and in the final chapter Owen writes of the communion of churches: 'our Lord Jesus Christ, in his infinite wisdom, hath constituted his churches in such a state and order as wherein none of them are able of themselves, always and in all instances, to attain all the ends for which they are appointed...We do believe that the <u>mutual communion of particular churches</u> amongst themselves, in an equality of power and order, though not of gifts and usefulness, is the only way appointed by our Lord Jesus Christ...for the attaining of the general end of all particular churches, which is the edification of the church catholic, in faith, love, and peace...'[38]

Synods, which are not (as in Browne) joint meetings of whole churches, but of messengers or delegates from the particular churches are entirely in harmony with the mind, though not with the express command, of Christ; and since 'the <u>end</u> of all particular churches is the edification of the <u>church catholic</u>, unto the glory of God in Christ,'[39] such gatherings are necessary - even inevitable. As to the power possessed by synods, this is threefold: 'The first is <u>declarative</u>, consisting in an authoritative teaching and declaring of the mind of God in the Scripture; the second is <u>constitutive</u>, appointing and ordaining things to be believed, or done and observed, by and upon its own authority; and, thirdly, <u>executive</u>, in acts of jurisdiction towards persons or churches.'[40] The deliverances of synods 'are to be received, owned and observed on the evidence of the mind of the Holy Ghost in them, and on the ministerial authority of the synod itself.'[41]

The Vice-Chancellor of Oxford University - perhaps not unnaturally - found it helpful to couch his arguments in a scholastic dress which lessens his impact upon the modern reader. The fact remains that Owen had a heart; and from time to time in his voluminous works his delight in the life of the covenanted fel-

lowship breaks through. So too does the challenge of that earthed sainthood which is Congregationalism's hallmark: 'If we find a person that is orderly admitted into church society, he is as certain and evident an object
of our love as if we saw him lying in the arms
of Christ. We walk by rule; He hath appointed
us to do so. Let none, then pretend that they
love the brethren in general, and love the
people of God, and love the saints, while
their love is not fervently exercised towards
those who are in the same church Society with
them. Christ hath given it you for a trial; He
will try your love at the last day by your de-
portment in that church wherein you are.'[42]

All the time their mentors were writing,
the saints were living; and in their local
covenants they gave verbal expression to the
bond which united them. That they did not do
so in exactly similar terms will become clear
if we consider a few examples. The 1629 covenant of the church at Salem, Massachusetts is
perhaps the simplest of all: 'We covenant with
the Lord and one with another; and do bind
ourselves in the presence of God, to walk together in all his ways, as he is pleased to
reveal himself unto us in his Blessed word of
truth.'[43] That the Salem members were not unaware of the challenge which saintly living
imposes is clear from their renewal of their
covenant in 1636:

> We whose names are hereunder written,
> members of the present Church of Christ
> in Salem, having found by sad experience
> how dangerous it is to sit loose to the
> Covenant we make with our God: and how
> apt we are to wander into bypaths, even
> to the losing of our first aims in
> entering into Church fellowship: Do

therefore solemnly in the presence of
the Eternal God, both for our own
comforts, and those which shall or may
be joined unto us, renew that Church
Covenant we find this Church bound unto
at their first beginning, viz:...[44]

In a very different political environment
the five men and three women who signed a covenant in Bury St. Edmunds on 16th May 1646
made no bones about their separatist motives:
'We being convinced in Conscience of the evil
of the Church of England...And being...fully
separated, not only from them, but also from
those who communicate with them either publicly or privately. We resolve by the grace of
God, not to return unto their vain inven-
tions...And we seeing not only the necessity
of this separation, but also the great need of
continuing in Christian fellowship... We do
therefore, together with our posterity, Covenant, to become a peculiar Temple for the Holy
Ghost to dwell in...and so to walk in all his
ways so far as he hath revealed unto us, or
shall reveal hereafter.'[45]

This church had but a short life. However,
two years later three of its members joined
with seven others, and on 21st December 1648
entered into a covenant in terms less shrill:
'We whose names here subscribed do resolve and
engage by the help of the Spirit of God to
walk in all the ways of God so far forth as He
hath revealed or shall reveal them unto us by
His word, and in all duties of love and watch-
fulness each to other as becomes a Church of
Christ.'[46]

Our next example (Cockermouth, 1651) makes
specific reference to church officers:

We poor worms, lost in Adam, being by

the grace of God, through the Spirit, called to be saints (conceiving it to be our duty to observe the gospel ordinances), for the future do agree together to walk as a people whom the Lord has chosen, an holy communion of saints; and we do mutually promise to watch over one another in the Lord, and to do all such things, according to our best light, that are required of a church in order, and to submit to our lawful officers, that shall from time be chosen out from among us. And this in the presence of the Lord we resolve and promise, hoping that of his goodness, and according to his wonted dealing with his people, he will carry us on to his praise.

Our final example is the 1687 covenant of the church at Angel Street, Worcester. It opens with a bold confession of faith in God the holy Trinity, and concludes thus: 'We do heartily take this one God for our only God, and our chief good, and this Jesus Christ for our only Lord, Redeemer, and Saviour, and this Holy Ghost for our Sanctifier; and the doctrine by him revealed and sealed by his miracles, and now contained in Holy Scriptures, we do take for the law of God, and the rule of our faith and life. And repenting unfeignedly of our sins we do resolve through the grace of God sincerely to obey him, both in holiness to God and righteousness to men, and in special love to the saints, and communion with them, against all the temptations of the devil, the world, and our own flesh, and this to the death.'

Thomas Badland, pastor, and forty-one members signed the Worcester covenant and, no

doubt, the presence or absence of a resident
minister (and there was none in Bury St.
Edmunds in 1646) influenced the terms in which
local covenants were expressed. Certainly the
Worcester covenant is more intensely theological than many; and it would seem that the
Worcester saints found it less necessary than
their earlier brethren to make out the case
for separation, or to note the differentiating
points of church order. The ecclesiological
case had been made; though perhaps the staunch
trinitarianism of the Worcester covenant suggests the need felt locally to guard against
Socinianising tendencies to which many Presbyterians and General Baptists, and some Congregationalists, were soon to succumb.[47]

Having reviewed writings and local covenants, it remains only to consider the most
formal of Congregational statements: the declarations and statements of faith. These are
the Cambridge [New England] Platform of 1646-8;
the Savoy Declaration of Faith and Order
(1658); and the Appendix to the latter (1688).
John Cotton was the leading light at
Cambridge; John Owen at the Savoy. We may
therefore expect that although the respective
climates in which the two declarations were
composed differed - the Americans were setting
down guidelines for church order in a New
World; the Savoy fathers were out to publicise
and justify their church order against its
rivals - the documents reveal a clear identity
of basic ecclesiological principle. With verbal amendments which inter alia brought Savoy
more into line with the phraseology of federal
theology, the Congregationalists of 1658 endorsed the doctrinal sections of the
Westminster Confession (approved by Parliament
on 20th June 1648[48]): but in their appended
Declaration of the Institution of Churches

they expounded the Congregational Way in thirty articles.

Chapter one of <u>Cambridge</u> declares that there is one immutable form of church government, prescribed in the Word of God: 'The parts of Government are prescribed in the word, because the Lord Jesus Christ the King and Law-giver of his Church, is no less faithful in the house of God than was Moses, who from the Lord delivered a <u>form and</u> pattern of Government to the Children of Israel in the Old Testament.' The parts of government are 'exactly described' in the Bible.[49] <u>Savoy</u> concurs, though with no explicit reference to the Old Testament, and with a more immediate focusing on the gathered church: those given to Christ by the Father 'he commandeth to walk together in particular Societies or Churches, for their mutual edification, and the due performance of that public Worship, which he requireth of them in this world.'[50]

<u>Cambridge</u> launches into a disquisition upon the catholic Church, militant and triumphant, visible and invisible, before declaring (without using the term 'gathered') that 'A Congregational-church, is by the institution of Christ a part of the Militant-visible-church, consisting of a company of Saints by calling, united into one body, by a holy covenant, for the public worship of God, and the mutual edification one of another, in the Fellowship of the Lord Jesus.'[51] The term 'saints' is then carefully defined: 'By Saints, we understand, 1. Such, as have not only attained the knowledge of the principles of Religion, and are free from gross and open scandals, but also do together with profession of their faith and Repentance, walk in blameless obedience to the word, so as that in charitable discretion they may be accounted Saints by calling, (though

perhaps some or more of them be unsound, and
hypocrites inwardly)...2.The children of such,
who are also holy.'[52] _Savoy_ concurs in its
Article VIII, except that it does not admit
the idea of the half-way covenant which the
second _Cambridge_ point affirms. The revision
of the Savoy _Declaration_ chapter XXVI by the
Massachusetts Synod of 1680 incorporates the
half-way covenant, and the Saybrook Platform
of 1708 reiterates the inclusion verbatim.

While _Cambridge_ says of particular churches
that 'each one is a distinct society of itself,'[53] _Savoy_ is much more explicit on the
principle of independency: 'Besides these particular Churches, there is not instituted by
Christ any Church more extensive or Catholic
entrusted with power for the administration of
his Ordinances, or the execution of any authority in his name.'[54] Not indeed that _any_
two or three gathered persons comprise the
church. The Savoy fathers advocate orderliness: 'A particular Church gathered and com-
pleted according to the mind of Christ, consists of Officers and Members: The Lord Jesus
Christ having given to his called ones (united
according to his appointment in Church-order)
Liberty and Power to choose Persons fitted by
the holy Ghost for that purpose, to be over
them, and to minister to them in the Lord.'[55]
Cambridge concurs, though in addition it makes
much of that officer whom _Savoy_ omits, the
ruling elder. His 'office is distinct from the
office of _Pastor and Teacher_,' and he is to
'join with the _Pastor and Teacher_ in those
acts of spiritual _Rule_ which are distinct from
the ministry of the word and Sacraments.'[56]
The New England churches came to be greatly
exercised over this office, of which Walker
opined that it 'occupied a position between
minister and the brethren sure to be full of

embarrassment and of no real use.'[57] Echoes of
this dispute were heard in England, and when
in 1691 the Congregational and Presbyterian
ministers joined in their Happy Union which,
owing to the fact that too many theological
cracks were papered over, so quickly proved
abortive, their Heads of Agreement included
this clause: 'Whereas divers are of opinion,
That there is also the Office of <u>Ruling El-
ders</u>, who labour not in <u>word and doctrine</u>; and
others think otherwise; We agree, That <u>this
difference</u> make no <u>breach</u> among us.'[58]

It may well be that <u>Savoy's</u> assertion of
independency is stronger than Owen himself
would have approved for to him, as we saw, the
catholic Church is prior to the particular
church. He would have been happier with the
place accorded by <u>Savoy</u> to synods, albeit
advisory ones only:

> In Cases of Difficulties or Differences,
> either in point of Doctrine or in Admin-
> istrations, wherein either the Churches
> in general are concerned, or any one
> Church in their Peace, Union, and Edifi-
> cation, or any Member or Members of any
> Church are injured in, or by any pro-
> ceeding in Censures, not agreeable to
> Truth and Order: it is according to the
> mind of Christ, that many Churches
> holding communion together, do by their
> Messengers meet in a Synod or Council,
> to consider and give their advice in, or
> about that matter in difference, to be
> reported to all the Churches concerned:
> Howbeit these Synods so assembled are
> not entrusted with any Church-Power
> properly so-called, or with any
> Jurisdiction over the Churches
> themselves, to exercise any Censures,

either over any Churches or Persons, or
to impose their determinations on the
Churches or Officers.

Besides these occasional Synods or
Councils, there are not instituted by
Christ any stated Synods in a fixed
Combination of Churches, or their Offi-
cers in lesser or greater Assemblies;
nor are there any Synods appointed by
Christ in a way of Subordination to one
another.[59]

Cambridge treats of inter-church fellowship
at considerably greater length, and is firmer
than Savoy that synods are not merely useful,
but right; and it is clearer on the spirit in
which synodical deliverances are to be received:

Although Churches be distinct, and
therefore may not be confounded one with
another: and equal, and therefore have
not dominion one over another: yet all
the churches ought to preserve Church-
communion one with another, because they
are all united unto Christ, not only as
a mystical, but as a political head;
whence is derived a communion suitable
thereto.

The communion of Churches is exercised sundry ways.

1. By way of mutual care in taking
thought for one another's welfare.

2. By way of Consultation with one
another, when we have occasion to
require the judgment and counsel of
other churches...

3...By way of admonition...

4....By way of participation at the
Lord's Table...

5....By way of <u>recommendation</u> when a
member of one church hath occasion to
reside in another church...
6...In case of <u>need</u>, to minister relief
and succour one unto another...

When a company of believers purpose
to gather into church fellowship, it is
requisite for their safer proceeding,
and the maintaining of the communion of
churches, that they signify their intent
unto the neighbour-churches...

Besides these several ways of communion, there is also a way of propagation
of churches...

Synods orderly assembled, and rightly
proceeding according to the pattern,
Acts 15, we acknowledge as the ordinance
of Christ...Elders and other Messengers...are the matter of a Synod...It
belongeth unto Synods and councils, to
debate and determine controversies of
faith, and cases of conscience...The
Synod's directions and determinations,
so far as consonant to the word of God,
are to be received with reverence and
submission...[60]

Both <u>Savoy</u> and <u>Cambridge</u>, though with differences of emphasis, represent attempts to
marry the ideas of local independence and ob-
ligatory wider fellowship within a coherent
ecclesiology. The successful accomplishment of
this task has been Congregationalism's perennial challenge.

By way of a bridge to our next chapter we
would note in conclusion that whereas
<u>Cambridge</u>, whose authors lived in a pioneering
land, quite naturally included church propagation among the objectives of inter-church
fellowship, more than one hundred and fifty

years were to elapse before such an idea was
to appear in formal English Congregational
declarations.

4. Towards Evangelic Congregationalism

In the light of the evidence so far adduced we can only endorse Dr. Nuttall's judgment that the notion of themselves as 'visible saints' was the 'controlling idea' of the Congregational fathers.[1] The ramifications of this position are manifold, and we have not been able fully to document or discuss them all. But clearly, the early Congregational Way runs counter to any hierarchical system of church government, whether episcopalian or presbyterian. Ministry is not a matter of priestly caste, but nor is it the case that in the church anyone may do anything. There <u>are</u> gifts, and it is for the church to recognise these. The stance is unsectarian in that it allows no 'new circumcision' to intervene between the Spirit's work of regeneration and the gathering of the people of God.[2] <u>All</u> who are called by, and gathered to and under Christ are the Church: hence the reluctance on the part of some later Congregationalists to conceive of a churchly body subsisting between the local church and the Church catholic. Consistently, the terms of church membership were response to the gospel and godly living, rather than 'outward' assent to 'man-made' creeds.[3] Certainly church membership was not conferred by domicile. But what if the saints ceased to behave as such? Enter church discipline, an obligation no doubt indulged in by

some of the fathers with excessive zeal. But
at their best they followed John Owen's way,
according to which the purpose of church cen-
sure was 'corrective, not vindictive - for
healing, not destruction;' and the onus was
upon the church to ensure that there was
'Prayer for the person cut off, admonition as
occasion is offered, compassion in his dis-
tressed state,' and 'readiness for the restoration of love in all the fruits of it.'[4] Baptism was for the children of the covenant; the
Lord's Supper was the covenant's sign and
seal; and inter-church fellowship was to be
enjoyed on a mutual basis as occasion demanded.

Lest we give the impression that Congregationalism was a theory and not a Way, we
repeat that underlying all was the conviction that if there is an absolute distinction
between those who are Christ's and those who
are not, it ought to show itself in a godly
walk. As Mackennal rightly said, 'It would be
like counting the sand to quote the numerous
cases where these early Congregationalists
assert that that only is a true Church of
Christ which is composed of spiritual men.'[5]
Undeniably there can be falsely pious, introspective, introverted Congregational churches;
but, then, there can be unworthy bishops and
unpleasantly autocratic synods: every ecclesiology is open to practical abuse. Certainly
some of those who attempted the saintly life
were well aware of the challenge it imposed
upon them. Thomas Goodwin (1600-80), member of
the Westminster Assembly and signatory to An
Apologeticall Narration, had to confess (in
words which if spoken today would sound
cheekily anti-ecumenical!), 'It is in my
spirit or "mind" only that I "serve the law"
of Independence: but in my "flesh" I serve the
law of Presbytery.'[6] But that many responded

sufficiently to the challenge of sainthood is
shown by the clear if grudging compliment paid
to the Independents by the Scottish Commis-
sioner Baillie in 1645: 'Of all the bye-paths
wherein the wanderers of our time are pleased
to walk, this is the most considerable, not
for the number but for the quality of the
erring persons therein. There be few of the
noted sects which are not a great deal more
numerous; but this way, what it wants in numbers, supplies by the weight of its followers.'[7]

We cannot overlook the fact that in making
the claims they did the early Congregational
fathers were, given the post-Restoration political climate, implicitly and at times ex-
plicitly, claiming religious freedom for themselves and, to a greater or lesser extent, for
others. At one extreme Jeremiah Burroughes, in
the interests of showing the similarity of
Congregationalists and Presbyterians, declared
in his Irenicum that 'we who are for a Congregational way do not hold absolute liberty for
all religions;'[8] at the other extreme John
Goodwin was more liberal in recognising that
those who demanded toleration for themselves
must be ready to concede it to others.[9]

It is hardly surprising that prior to the
passing of the Toleration Act of 1689 Congregationalism could not, even had it so wished,
have provided itself with a nationwide organization. The remarkable fact is that political
and social obstacles notwithstanding, there
was a real measure of mutual intercourse,
especially between ministers, in various lo-
calities. The best known example of this is
Richard Baxter's ecclesiologically flexible
Worcestershire Agreement of May 1652. Baxter's
lead was followed by Adam Martindale and his
Cheshire colleagues (October 1653); by the

ministers of Cumberland and Westmorland
(1656); and later, after a taste of Parlia-
mentary Presbyterianism, by those in the counties of Norfolk, Essex and Devonshire.

Some of these Associations, like that in
Devon and Cornwall, met for the ordination of
ministers, though Baxter's did not.[10] In the
north-west in 1674, Thomas Jollie, not without
difficulty, succeeded in summoning messengers
from churches in Yorkshire, Lancashire and
Cheshire to a conference which endorsed the
Savoy Declaration;[11] and in May 1680 he at-
tended a three-day meeting for ministers and
'some select brethren' held at Woodchurch,
Yorkshire. The meeting discussed 'the accommo-
dation and association of churches.'[12] In New
England the first ministerial association was
formed on a voluntary basis at Cambridge,
Massachussetts in 1690, and in 1709 consociations of ministers and lay representatives
were instituted in Connecticut.

March 17th-18th 1691 saw the first meeting,
at Tiverton, of the Exeter Assembly which, as
well as administering a Fund for the education
of ministers and the relief of the widows and
orphans of ministers, concerned itself with
ordinations and questions of church discipline. Its composition was entirely ministerial, and largely Presbyterian. Certainly the
Independent John Ashwood of Exeter saw no need
to acquaint the Association with his participation in a service of ordination at
Bridport.[13]

These Associations survived for varying
lengths of time. Although the Happy Union of
1691 came to nought, other Associations proved
more durable. The Exeter Association continues to this day; and the Lancashire Union was
not formed until 1693, after the dissolution
of its London counterpart.

From the point of view of the Congregational idea of the Church, it is clear that
whether they comprised ministers only, or ministers and laymen, no vital principle was com-
promised by the Associations, for they were
voluntary, non-executive bodies. The same may
be said of the similar associations formed
during the first half of the eighteenth century. Among these were the London Board of Congregational Ministers (1727), and the Associations encouraged and influenced by Philip
Doddridge. Following a visit in 1741 to the
Associations of Protestant Dissenting Ministers in Norfolk and Suffolk Doddridge wrote a
letter advocating his view 'that neighbouring
ministers, in one part of our land and another, especially in this country, should enter
into associations, to strengthen the hands of
each other by united consultations and
prayer...'[14] A year later he enquired at the
Northamptonshire Association meeting 'Whether
something might not be done in most of our
congregations towards assisting in the propagation of Christianity abroad, and spreading
it in some of the darker parts of our own
land.' Nor was Doddridge the first to adum-
brate an evangelistic motive for association.
In 1728 Independent ministers of Derbyshire,
Nottinghamshire and Sheffield addressed themselves to the question, 'What means are to be
used for the Reviving and Promoting Primitive
Christianity?' and they called for 'Solemn
Prayer to God in each Respective Church for
the Pouring forth of the Spirit.'[15] The recol-
lection of such things is a salutary dissuasive to the view that in the eighteenth century all was black before John Wesley rode into
view.

The hymns of Watts and Doddridge constitute
a further dissuasive, and one which was of the

greatest <u>practical</u> importance ecclesiologically. The saints used hymns as means of praise and testimony; and they were, in turn, fed by them. There can be little doubt, for example, that a local church's sense of corporate, covenanted identity was enhanced when, with Watts, its members affirmed their belief that

> The whole creation is Thy charge,
>   but saints are Thy peculiar care.

When Doddridge, echoing <u>Exodus</u> xxviii:29, declared that

> The names of all his saints he bears
>   Deep graven on his heart,

the Congregationalists humbly prayed

> So, gracious Saviour, on my breast
>   May Thy dear name be worn...

All was of grace; and that distinction of eternal significance between those who are Christ's and those who are not - the distinction upon which the Congregational ecclesiology rests - was propouned by Watts thus:

> The sovereign will of God alone
>   Creates us heirs of grace,
> Born in the image of His Son,
>   A new, peculiar race.

There is Calvinism at its most personal, and at its least individualistic. Again, it is surely not fanciful to suppose that behind the following familiar lines there lies Doddridge's own experience:

> O happy day that fixed my choice
>> On Thee, my Saviour and my God...
> 'Tis done, the great transaction's done;
>> I am my Lord's, and He is mine;
> He drew me, and I followed on,
>> Charmed to confess the voice divine.

In Job Orton's edition of Doddridge's Hymns (1755) the hymn just quoted is headed, 'Rejoicing in our Covenant Engagements to God.' Nor could that covenant, once made, be broken - as Watts reminded his fellow Christians:

> Saints by the power of God are kept
>> Till the salvation come;
> We walk by faith, as strangers here,
>> Till Christ shall call us home.

A glance at two British works, accompanied by some doctrinal and American allusions, will enable us to take stock of the position of the Congregational idea of the Church by the middle of the eighteenth century. First, Robert Bragge's Church Discipline according to its Ancient Standard, As it was Practis'd in Primitive Times (1739). Bragge informs us that the primitive Church was 'Gospel-like or Evangelical...The original Form of Gospel Churches was not carnal and worldly, but heavenly and spiritual.'[16] The regenerate alone were church members; the churches were not national but congregational; and, since they were upheld by Christ they had no need of the civil magistrate's support. Towards the end of his book he has much to say concerning the necessity of church fellowship, but it is all to do with the benefits and obligations respecting the association of individual believers with particular churches. He does not mention interchurch association.

It was perhaps partly because of this lack
that Howel Harris could not rest content with
Independency. On 2nd December 1741 he wrote in
his diary: 'I see I know nothing about church
government, but it seems that Independency to
me is not right.'[17] No doubt Harris's difficulty was compounded by the fact that there
was no viable Presbyterian alternative to hand
for comparison. For, as is well known, except
in Lancashire, London and certain eastern
counties, the Presbyterian polity had not
proved possible - nor was it always desired by
Presbyterians - to put into practice. Hence,
by the middle of the eighteenth century Presbyterianism, if becoming more generally heter-
odox than Congregationalism, was for most
practical purposes independent in government,
with the important proviso that the _basis_ of
the independence was not as in Congregationalism. A ruling oligarchy tended to assume
the obligations fulfilled in Congregationalism
by the gathering of saints. Some erstwhile
Presbyterian churches became avowedly Congregational; that at Ravenstonedale, for example,
passed through many vicissitudes until it was
reorganised on the decidedly Congregational
plan in 1811.[18]

It is interesting to note that as regards
polity the judgment of Cotton Mather applies,
though for opposite reasons, to both the American and the British situation: 'The Differences between Presbyterian and Congregational
seem hardly to be known in this country.'[19]
But whereas, as we have said, the edges were
blurred by the absence in England of a dis-
tinctly Presbyterian structure, in America
they were blurred by the organisational necessities entailed by that zeal for mission to
which we earlier alluded. Although Mather had
to grant that the various proposals respecting

Associations had yet to be fully complied with
(and Massachussetts, for example, always gave
greater place to the notion of autonomy, while
Connecticut emphasised consociation),[20] he
could still say that 'the Country is full of
Associations, formed by the Pastors in their
several Vicinities, for the Prosecution of
Evangelical Purposes.'[21]

As might be expected, the doctrinal dis-
putes of the eighteenth century had at least a
local influence upon polity. Sometimes, as a
congregation's theology changed its denominational allegiance, sooner or later changed.
Thus, for example, the old Presbyterian foundations at Kendal and Stourbridge became Unitarian; and among erstwhile Congregational
churches which travelled the same road were a
number in Cheshire, including Hale, Knutsford,
Macclesfield and Nantwich. On the other hand,
a church might find itself in a succession of
denominations because of its <u>refusal</u> to succumb to 'advanced' thought. Thus, the church
at Carlton, Bedfordshire, Calvinistic since
the seventeenth century, has successively been
Congregational, and is now Strict Baptist.
Again, the variety of High Calvinism which
Joseph Hussey came to espouse - a Calvinism
which prohibited him from freely offering the
gospel - presupposed the view that saints
alone could have the fulness of the gospel
preached to them.[22] (Some have even attempted
to make a Hussey out of Isaac Watts by offering an exclusivist interpretation of his
line to the effect that the saints comprise a
'garden walled around.' But this is to overlook the particular point that in the same
hymn Watts makes it plain that the influence
of the saints is to permeate the world around
them; and it is to challenge the general point
that if ever the line between the saints and

the world is disallowed the Congregational,
not to mention the New Testament, idea of the
Church is undermined). Finally, what was often
referred to as 'the Socinian blight' prompted
a more decidedly doctrinal stance in some of
the local covenants and associations of the
eighteenth century. Thus, according to its
Church Book, when Manchester's Cannon Street
Independent church moved into its new premises
in 1762, the Westminster Confession was pre-
fixed to 'The Constitution, Officers, Ordinances, Rules and Orders of a Gospel Church,'
the whole 'to be afresh assented to, and
faithfully followed, by all those that are
already in the Church or may hereafter be
received into it.' And in a document relating
to an attempt to form an Association in
Manchester on 2nd June 1784 it was made clear
that 'though a diversity of expression upon
some points is unavoidable, yet there must be
a general harmony and agreement with reference
to our views of Scripture and the doctrines
mentioned by Calvinistic Independent
churches.'[23]

Our conclusion must be that while general
doctrinal debates caused local shifts of denominational allegiance, and influenced the
wording of covenants and constitutions, they
did not entail the redefinition of the fundamental principles of Congregational polity.
What was to re-contextualise, if not to modi-
fy, those principles was the fanning into a
flame of the evangelical motive which had been
sporadically voiced prior to 1750.

The second book to which we refer is
Matthias Maurice's allegorical Social Religion
Exemplify'd in an Account of the First Settle-
ment of Christianity in the City of Caerludd
(1750). The author presents a dialogue in
defence of the ideal (that is, the Congrega-

tional) church government. He goes further than Bragge in his advocacy of synods for mutal advice; but when a local church receives the deliverance of a synod, 'if anything therein appears to them contrary to the revealed Will of their Lord Jesus, they are not bound to submit thereto, but peaceably dissent therein from the Thoughts of their Brethren, and do in it as well as they can.'[24] When, at the end of the work Christophilus thanks Epenetus for the 'edifying Account' he has given, and prays: 'The Eternal Spirit fill us, fill our Families, fill the Churches, and hasten the Time to fill the Earth with the Knowledge of the Glory our Redeemer, as the Waters cover the Sea. Amen,'[25] we have yet another earnest of that evangelical note which was to strengthen the desire for association during the last quarter of the century.

We do not wish to suggest that the obligation to evangelise was felt by all parts of the land concurrently. There were time-lags as between different areas, and ebbs and flows within the same area. The articles of the mooted Lancashire Association of 1784 provided that 'Any minister has a right to propose any overture or plan for promoting the success of the Gospel in any desolate corners...:'[26] but the Association constituted in Bolton on 7th June 1786 was not overtly evangelistic. Its objects include mutual advice and discipline on the basis of 'evangelical doctrine, as maintained by the reformed churches.' The fact that 'it be not the intention of this Association to infringe in the least upon the liberties of Christian Churches' is made plain. But to concerted evangelistic outreach there is no reference.[27] The same could not be said of the group which met on 22nd August 1798 at Tintwistle, Cheshire, 'for the purpose of

promoting a more friendly intercourse among
ministers and Christian brethren, and of con-
sulting together for the wider extension of
the gospel.'[28] The fruit of this meeting was
the Itinerant Society of 1801. The Lancashire
Union itself was constituted in 1806. The
Union Plan contains the following consecutive
proposals: 'That it shall not interfere, directly or indirectly, with the independent
rights and discipline of any particular
church. That its object shall be the introduction and spread of the Gospel, according to
the Congregational order, especially in the
most populous parts of the county to which
the Union extends.'[29] Here, side by side, are
the ancient platform and the modern impetus of
denominational Congregationalism.[30]

The Lancashire Union was not the first in
the field. That honour goes to Hampshire
(1781). Devonshire came next (1782); Kent in
1791, Warwickshire in 1793 and Dorset in 1795.
All of these emphasized the necessities of
evangelism, and it is not without significance that Burder of Warwickshire and Bogue of
Hampshire were founding fathers of the London
Missionary Society (1795). Indeed it was the
formation of the overseas mission which
prompted many, like James Bowden of Tooting to
ask, 'What of the rural areas at home?' Hence,
inter alia, the Surrey Mission Society (1797),
predecessor of the Surrey Union. Meanwhile
Unions had been formed in 1796 in Shropshire
and Somerset, and by 1815 thirteen other areas
had followed suit.

In 1808 a General Congregational Union was
formed, and gradually attempts were made
towards the establishment of a Congregational
Union of England and Wales. The goal was
reached on 10th May 1831. We need not pursue
the history of the Union in detail,[31] though

we must draw out the ecclesiological implications of such a Union, and we must note the reactions to it. There was widespread agreement that the saints must evangelise,[32] and the majority accepted that such work inevitably brought with it an increase of bureaucracy. At this point the respective claims of fellowship and independence were pressed, and it was to be about one hundred and thirty years before the Congregationalists finally agreed a theory explanatory of their increasingly <u>corporately</u>-churchly activities.

Two further results of the Evangelical Revival remain to be noted. First, the Revival led to the formation of a number of local churches which came to be absorbed into the Congregational family. This statement applies not only to many churches of the Countess of Huntingdon's Connexion, but also to a number of other churches which at first were independent with a small 'i'. Among the latter were some gathered under the preaching of students itinerating from Lady Huntingdon's College at Trevecca, and from other similarly Calvinistic and evangelical institutions.[33] Conditions were fluid, and there was movement in the other direction as well, as when those dissenting churches in the Ayron valley, who looked for leadership to Thomas Grey, went over to Methodism.[34]

Secondly, the Revival encouraged the restoration, for a time, of the practice of requiring the saints to 'give in' an 'experience' - that is, to relate God's dealings with their souls - on reception into membership of the church. The question whether or not a definite conversion experience of the evangelical type was a precondition of membership was keenly debated up to 1800. Among the ramifications of this debate was the question whether a student training for the ministry must be, in the evangelical sense, a converted person. Dr. John Pye Smith answered in the affirmative, as did teachers in, and supporters of, Homerton Academy and those connected with such academies as Rotherham, Gosport and Newport, which had been spawned by the Revival. But at Hoxton, Wymondley and elsewhere the requirement, in keeping with the older dissenting tradition, was not made. The divergence here was an aspect of that wider suspicion of 'enthusiasm' on the part of representatives of the older dissent, which had even led Isaac Watts and the Coward Trustees to reprove Doddridge for the endorsement he gave to George Whitefield.[35]

Circumstances and opinions varied across the land, but by 1821 a writer, lamenting the less than challenging way in which membership was presented to those who sought it, recalled that once 'No person used to be admitted into the church without being examined as to knowledge and experience publicly, before a considerable congregation; and, yet, it was scarcely ever known, that any person was deterred from offering himself as a candidate for communion, on account of the strict mode of admission.'[36] To this theme we shall return in the next chapter.

5. Denominational Congregationalism

It would be an over-simplification to say that from the formation of the Congregational Union we have the idea of fellowship expressed on the one hand, local autonomy on the other, and that what is common to both is the concept of sainthood. The fact is that sainthood it-self came to be variously construed. Some justified autonomy - even individualism - on the ground that saints are <u>locally</u> gathered. Others, following Owen (consciously or other-wise), argued that because sainthood is cath-olic, fellowship comes before locality. Oth-ers, again, held that precisely because of the catholicity of the Church, there could be no such thing as a Church in the denominational sense intervening between the local church and the catholic Church; nor could they find any such entity in the New Testament. Numerous variations were played upon these themes, and it is with this confused and confusing score that we must now grapple. Our point of depar-ture may properly be the 'Principles of Church Order and Discipline' which were appended to the moderately Calvinistic 'Principles of Religion' adopted by the Union in May 1833:

> 1. The Congregational Churches hold .it to be the will of Christ that true believers should voluntarily assem-ble together to observe religious

religious ordinances, to promote mutual edification and holiness, to perpetuate and propagate the Gospel in the world, and to advance the glory and worship of God, through Jesus Christ; and that each society of believers, having these objects in view in its formation, is properly a Christian church.

2. They believe that the New Testament contains...all the articles of faith necessary to be believed, and all the principles of order and discipline requisite for constituting and governing Christian societies...

3. They acknowledge Christ as the only Head of the Church, and the officers of each church under Him, as ordained to administer His laws impartially to all; and their only appeal, in all questions touching their religious faith and practice, is to the sacred Scriptures.

4. They believe that the New Testament authorises every Christian church to elect its own officers, to manage all its own affairs, and to stand independent of, and irresponsible to, all authority, saving that only of the Supreme and Divine Head of the Church, the Lord Jesus Christ.

5. They believe that the only officers placed by the apostles over individual churches are the bishops or pastors and the deacons...

6. They believe that no persons should be received as members of Christian churches, but such as make a credible profession of Christianity, are living according to its precepts,

and attest a willingness to be
subject to its discipline...

9. They believe that the power of a
    Christian church is purely spiritual
    and should in no way be corrupted by
    union with temporal or civil power.

10. They believe that it is the duty of
    Christian churches to hold communion
    with each other...and to co-operate
    for the promotion of the Christian
    cause; but that no church, or union
    of churches, has any right or power
    to interfere with the faith or dis-
    cipline of any other church further
    than to separate from such as, in
    faith or practice, depart from the
    Gospel of Christ...

12. They believe that church officers,
    whether bishops or deacons, should
    be chosen by the free voice of the
    church...

13. They believe that the fellowship of
    every Christian church should be so
    liberal as to admit to communion in
    the Lord's Supper all whose faith
    and godliness are, on the whole, un-
    doubted, though conscientiously dif-
    fering in points of minor impor-
    tance...[1]

Here we have the declaration that the
Church comprises saints; that the Bible is the
supreme authority for faith and practice; that
local churches are voluntary assemblies of believers; that local churches are to appoint
officers, to be untrammelled by civil alli-
ances, and to participate in the work and
witness of the wider fellowship of churches.
The most important addition to Savoy here is
the evangelistic motive; the most significant

omission is any reference to synods. When the
Constitution of the Union was subsequently
twice amended, there was no withdrawing from
the principle that 'the Union shall not, in
any case, assume legislative authority, or
become a court of appeal.'[2] In all this lie
the seeds of that tension between autonomy and
fellowship of which ripples are felt to this
day.[3] Dr. Peel expressed the paradox with
which Congregationalists have ever wrestled
thus: 'If anything is to live, it must be
organised; and yet organisation kills it.'[4]

That America was not unaware of the tension
was made clear at the second assembly of the
International Congregational Council (1899):
'ecclesiastical discrepancy between men who
put independence first and fellowship second,
and men who put fellowship first and independence second, may result in practical dead-
lock. When the starboard oar is pulling hard
and the port oar is backing water, the boat
simply turns round and round; or, to drop a
poor figure - and adopt a poorer one probably
- we all agree that both independence and fellowship shall ride in the same carriage; but
which shall drive? While you are settling that
practical question the practical horse stands
practically still.'[5]

To begin in the easiest place: we have
found none in the period 1831-1957 who denied
that the Church comprises saints, and many who
have emphasized the idea. Indeed, the idea was
underlined by some because of the very success
of the Evangelical Revival in bringing into
the churches those who had at best been embryo
saints. It was this influx of interested but
not fully committed hearers which impelled
William Roby towards Independency. Whilst
minister of the Countess of Huntingdon Church
at Wigan he found that exhortation was his

only weapon against those who came intoxicated to the Lord's table. He sought to 'form a Christian Church, composed of approved Christian professors and subject to Christian discipline, to whom the ordinance of the Supper should be confined.'[6] His church officers would not, however, agree to fence the table. For the time being Roby's loyalty to his flock kept him at Wigan, but at last, finding that he could tolerate the compromise no longer, he resigned, and then accepted the pastorate of the Congregational church at Cannon Street, Manchester.

The requirements exacted of hearers who desired church membership were in many cases less stringent than hitherto. Whereas oral profession of faith before the church had been customary, now the writing of a statement, or even simply evidence of a godly walk, was deemed sufficient. When those thus received had not enjoyed an upbringing within the covenanted fellowship it was only to be expected that their ecclesiological notions should be vague. Again, the urgency to press for conversion, together with the increasingly introspective approach of many evangelistic preachers, prompted a writer in the first volume of the popular Christian's Penny Magazine (1846) to exalt the objective, and to recall his readers to the Godward implications of their sainthood:

> The ultimate design of Christian fellowship is, the promotion of the Divine glory. This great object is accomplished by that voluntary act which brings the body of believers together into fellowship. Their withdrawment from the world, their union with each other, their observance of his ordinances, and obedi-

ence to his laws, are practical and visible demonstrations of subjection to the
authority of the Son of God; just as
declining to enter that fellowship is a
practical and visible contempt of his
authority. The churches of Christ are
God's witnesses among the profane popu-
lation of this sinful world.[7]

Here, two hundred years on, is that understanding of separation to which John Robinson
and others had subscribed. Earlier in the same
volume there appears an article entitled,
'Persons of whom a Church Consists,' which begins: 'A Christian church is an entirely spiritual structure. Every member of it is the
fruit of spiritual operation. By the Spirit he
is quickened, illumined, taught, and moulded
to accord with the foundation-stone upon
which, by faith, the church is built.'[8] The
dangers of 'knowingly blending ungodly men
with the faithful 'having been adverted to,
the writer cries, 'Oh! it will be a happy day
when it can be generally said of the ministers
of the gospel that they "teach my people the
difference between the holy and profane"...The
church has accommodated too much to the world,
and thus swelling her numbers, she has called
it prosperity; but such apparent prosperity
has often led to ultimate ruin...She will rise
with the freshness of the morning, and come
forth bright as the sun, clear as the moon,
and terrible as an army with banners.'[9]

Alongside this soul-searching on the part
of some we find others indulging in what, with
the benefit of hindsight, we can only describe
as Congregational triumphalism: 'Our Principles, as Congregationalists, are appreciated
more than ever. They are better known; they
are more philosophically and appropriately

regarded; they are more highly estimated...It is seen by many who entertained very dissimilar views formerly, that our principles of religion are of the most grave, enlightened, and noble character - and that our ecclesiastical plity is marked by its wisdom, its sagacity, its breadth, its usefulness, its admirable simplicity.'[10]

In America a quarter of a century later H.M. Dexter was demonstrating why Congregationalism 'is better than any other form of church government.' (Meanwhile, for example, his Irish contemporary Professor T.M. Witherow was asking, 'The Apostolic Church: Which Is it?' and giving the unequivocal answer, 'The Presbyterian'[11]). As late as 1902 Dugald Macfadyen could opine that 'To the Congregational churches of today has descended the privilege of witnessing to an ideal of the Christian Church so beautiful, historic, fruitful, and true, that it is worth pleading for with passionate conviction, working for with foresight and energy, and preserving by all the resources of organisation.'[12]

Some of Macfadyen's fellows night well have queried the extent to which what Congregationalism _really_ stood for could be preserved by all the resources of organisation. Certainly exponents of the spiritual foundation of Congregationalism were not lacking. In his manual of _Our Principles_ G.B. Johnson declared, 'We believe that none but godly men should be united into a Church.'[13] Said Dexter, 'Congregationalism is preeminently the spiritual polity. It is less than nothing and vanity if the power of a godly life be not behind it.'[14] There is, contended the leader writer in _The Congregationalist_, 'a distinction of infinite gravity between the regenerate and the unregenerate,' and this distinc-

tion is frankly drawn every time a 'separate'
church is established.[15] Churches formed on
such a basis, said J.A. Macfadyen in his Autumnal Address to the Congregational Union in
1882, have faithfully upheld evangelical
truth; have solved the problem of Christian
union; have maintained the true dignity of
man; and have been impelled upon mission.[16]
Charles A. Berry reiterated the point in his
Chairman's Address of 1879; 'Personal salvation is essential to churchmanship, not
churchmanship to personal salvation;' and because it maintains this Congregationalism is
'essential, spiritual, positive, permanent:
not accidental, political, negative, ephemer-
al.'[17] R.W. Dale agreed, and as he contem-
plated religious establishments then and now
he wrote of the Pilgrim Fathers that 'They
disapproved... of the constitution of the
Church of England, of its bishops, and of the
government exercised over it by the Queen and
Parliament. They judged it by its own Articles, which declare that "a church is a congregation of faithful men," as well as by the
New Testament, and denied it to be a true
Church at all, though there were many excel-
lent Christian persons in it; and to that
denial I firmly hold.'[18]

Positively, Dale informed the first meeting
of the International Congregational Council
(1891) that 'The Church - this is the Congregational ideal - is a society, larger or
smaller, consisting of those who have received
the Divine life, and who, with whatever incon-
stancy and whatever failures, are endeavouring
to live in the power of it...The responsibilities and the corresponding powers attributed
to the commonality of Christian people are
directly related to the assumption that they
have received the life that dwells in Christ,

and that they are one with Him.'[19] Dale's description of the gathering of such saints in
church meeting has the status of the classical: 'to be at a church meeting - apart from
any prayer that is offered - any hymn that is
sung, any words that are spoken, is for me one
of the chief means of grace. To know that I am
surrounded by men and women who dwell in God,
who have received the Holy Ghost, with whom I
am to share the eternal righteousness, and
eternal rapture of the great life to come,
this is blessedness. I breathe a Divine air. I
am in the new Jerusalem...I rejoice in the joy
of Christ over those whom He has delivered
from eternal death and lifted up into the
light and glory of God. The Kingdon of God is
there.'[20]

Implicit here, as also in J.A. Macfadyen,
Berry and others, is the view that the church
does not comprise saints conceived as isolated
individuals. It is a fellowship of saints -
though when Dr. J. Vernon Bartlet spoke of the
Church as a 'corporate spiritual personal-
ity,'[21] he was using then-fashionable psychological jargon of which the fathers were, happily, innocent. The point was never more engagingly made than by Bernard Lord Manning:

You say you love Christ's Church. Well,
here it is: Tom, Dick, Harry, and the
rest; a funny lot of lame ducks, but
they carry out the conditions we have
laid down. They are not very good. They
are not very nice. But they have, in
their own odd ways, heard Christ's call.
They have trusted in Christ on His
Cross. They have made a covenant with
God, and so joined themselves to the
saved society with Him. It is little use
your feeling mystical sympathy with

St. Francis who is dead, with St. Some-
body Else who never existed, with men of
good will all over the world whom you
are quite safe from meeting. If you do
not love your brothers whom you have
seen - Tom, Dick, Harry - you cannot, in
fact, love those brothers (whom you call
the Church) whom you have not seen.
Congregationalism makes us not flabby
and sentimental about the Church, but
tells us to get down to it in practice.[22]

There is earthed - even earthy - sainthood
if ever we saw it! And Manning realised that
he was but updating the very words of Owen
which we quoted in the chapter before last.

Dugald Macfadyen thought that Congregationalism was destined to go from strength to
strength, and he did not hesitate to draw un-
favourable comparisons: 'It is because the
Congregational system gives full room to the
redemptive and constructive powers of the
Gospel to do their own work, that we believe
it will ultimately justify its right to be
regarded as a more valid, because more Christian, organisation of Christian communities
than the Anglican.'[23] Men otherwise as different from each other as Cardinal Newman and
Herbert Spencer (both of whom, in other con-
nections, were roundly condemned by Congregationalists) are invoked in support. As Spencer
said, a process of development will go on
'from indefinite incoherent homogeneity to
definite coherent heterogeneity of structure
and function.'[24] Any implied arrogance in
Macfadyen's presentation of his case is miti-
gated by the fact that he recognises the abil-
ity of churches to grow _away_ from Christ, and
hopes for 'the conversion of our own churches

to Congregationalism as the highest and most
spiritual form of churchmanship.'[25]

Dr. F.J. Powicke was prominent in pleading
for spirituality before machinery in churchly
affairs;[26] and Peel typically averred, 'only
one thing makes a church - not officers, not
creeds, not sacraments, but believing men and
women, those who have been saved by Christ and
gathered together into a fellowship of the
Divine life.'[27] Some, however, came increasingly to feel that while the spiritual life
was of supreme importance, emphasis upon it
could not be said to be the differentia of
Congregationalism. Other denominations shared
the spiritual ideal. Thus, Benjamin
Nightingale took issue with Drs. Powicke and
Peel, and claimed autonomy as Congregationalism's distinctive par excellence, as we shall
see.

No doubt the idea that the church comprises
saints holds dangers. Paramount among these is
that emphasis upon the fellowship of believers
can, though it need, and ought, not, detract
from the realisation that the Christian re-
sponds to God's prevenient, gracious call. In
a word, believing can become a 'work.'[28]
Again, 'saints' can be arrogant and falsely
pious, though they need not be so, and have no
reason to be so. In this connection it is
pleasant to record that when Caleb Warhurst
and the Cannon Street members renewed their
covenant in 1760, both pastor and people acknowledged that 'They have not kept so close
to this Faith and Order of the Gospel as they
ought to have Done.'[29] Pitfalls apart, when
making a statement to the World Council of
Churches in 1951, Congregationalists were
willing to go back to their first major Declaration in saying that Congregationalists
'accept the statement of the Savoy Declaration

of 1658 that "members of these churches are
saints by calling, visibly manifesting and
evidencing in and by their profession and
walking their obedience unto that call of
Christ."'[30]

So much the spiritual emphasis, and for
sainthood. Our reference to Benjamin
Nightingale prompts us now to take up the emphasis upon local autonomy which was regarded
by many during the period under review as Congregationalism's distinctive. It is proper to
point out that to many, local independence and
autonomy were but the inevitable outcome of
their belief in the church qua saints. Others,
however, gave their independency an isolation-
ist turn - especially in face of the growth of
denominational organisational structures. Of
the latter S.T. Porter is among the more extreme examples. With experience of both the
English and Scottish Unions behind him he
announced that 'in respect of the leaders of
both associations...there is not one of them
who is trusted by his brethren.'[31]

Earlier, some pseudonymous brethren had
argued pro and con the names 'Congregational'
and 'Independent.' In defence of the latter it
was claimed that 'Independency certainly does
restrict the management of church affairs to
the parties most interested, and thus raises
an effectual - I may say the only effectual
barrier against priestly domination, but there
is nothing in the system of independency
rightly understood, which the most Catholic
spirit could feel a restraint.'[32] Again, Dr.
Stoughton recalls John Nelson Goulty, who
'felt immensely jealous of all proceedings
which threatened ecclesiastical liberty, which
trenched in the smallest degree upon the right
of churches to manage their own affairs, without the interference of extraneous authority...

Hence he was alarmed when the Union was projected, and argued against it might and main. He saw in it a Trojan horse full of mischief; predicted the rise of spiritual assumption; suspected the approach of a controlling money power; deprecated the perils of centralization; and strove to hark back his brethren from deceitful bye-ways to the well and wisely trodden paths of the old dissent.'[33] John Griffin of Portsea and Mr. Guyer of Ryde were, Stoughton thought, likeminded. All such must have been greatly heartened by Dr. Robert Vaughan's Address to the Union in 1841, in which the authority of the Chair was placed behind their fears.

Thirty years on an Independent could lament that 'The most recent fetter, whereby it is unwittingly intended to unfit Independency for the age, by imposing bondage and introducing confusion, is a resolution lately carried by the "London Board of Ministers," and strongly advocated by the "English Independent," and is to the effect that it is highly advisable that before any minister be recognised there shall be a Conference composed of ministers and delegates of local Churches to give him the opportunity of satisfying them about his moral character, his views of truth, the reasons for his accepting the charge, and whatever else may be deemed necessary. Realise the elements of which such assemblies will be composed, and say if they will not sometimes be a complete farce; sometimes a torturing inquisition; and sometimes the scene of discussion ending in disastrous dissension.'[34] In face of such encroachments the author could not keep silent (though he did preserve his anonymity). Though less megalomanic, The Congregationalist agreed that for a church 'to remit the ultimate government of its affairs to an external authority

is an act which corresponds very closely to
the blind surrender of our individual life to
the control of a priest.'[35] In his History of
English Congregationalism, the editor of The
Congregationalist, R.W. Dale, set down con-
cisely the views which he had expounded at
length in his Manual of Congregational principles (1884):

> 'Congregationalism' denotes a positive
> theory of the organisation and powers of
> Christian Churches. This theory main-
> tains (1) That Churches are not in the
> strictest sense of the words 'voluntary
> societies,' but societies founded by
> Christ Himself, to which it is His will
> that all those who believe in Him should
> belong. (2) That in every Christian
> Church the will of Christ is the supreme
> authority, and that in the reception and
> exclusion of members, in the election of
> officers, in the conduct of worship, and
> in every other church act, it is to be
> implicitly obeyed. (3) That there is an
> infinite contrast between those who re-
> ceive the Lord Jesus Christ as the Son
> of God and the Saviour of the human
> race, and those who do not; and that
> only those who have so received Him
> should be members of Christian Churches.
> (4) That by the will of Christ all the
> members of a Christian Church - not the
> officers only - are directly responsible
> to Him for maintaining His authority.
> And (5) That as an inference from. the
> last principle, every society of Chris-
> tians organised for Christian worship,
> instruction, and fellowship is a Chris-
> tian church and is Independent of exter-
> nal control.[36]

There is nothing here positively in favour of inter-church co-operation; still less anything respecting synods. But Dale would have been the first to agree with these words:

> Let none imagine that because the churches of the Independent faith and order are thus distinct form each other, and individually competent to the management of their own affairs, that therefore they are divided among themselves, and alienated in heart, in fellowship, or in worship, from their brethren of similar communions in different places. Far otherwise...The fact is, that there is no general division of the Christian church in which more order and substantial agreement are found: and amongst the different parts, or constituent assemblies of which, greater unity prevails.[37]

Like many others, Dale had little patience with individualism, and he regretted the extent to which Congregationalism had 'exaggerated and misinterpreted the great Protestant principle that religion is an affair that lies altogether between a man and his Maker,' and had forgotten that 'isolation is not the law of the religious life.'[38] To Dale the local church was the Church catholic; for 'what is affirmed of the universal Church appears in the New Testament to be affirmed of every organised assembly of Christain men.'[39] For all that, the general thrust of Dale's position is that inter-church co-operation is <u>not prevented</u> by the New Testament or within Congregationalism. He does not attempt a fully-fledged theology of such co-operation. Among others who fought individualism was C.A. Berry:

'Congregationalists,' he declared, 'are churchmen, as opposed to individualists. We are living members of an organism, not loose atoms wandering in eternal isolation.'[40] The same conviction prompted Dr. G.S. Barrett to warn the International Congregational Council against the 'unlovely independency of some churches' which denied that 'The manifold trees in the garden of the Lord are all rooted in the same kindly soil. We do not even grow in grace alone. We "are builded together for a holy temple in the Lord."'[41] The majority of the spokesmen would have endorsed John Brown's view that 'While maintaining that internal freedom essential to true church life, no church has a right to do just as it likes, to be as isolated, as angular, as contentious as it pleases. If it is a church of Christ at all it is a member of the body of Christ, and therefore what it does affects the character and reputation of the whole...It is here we come upon a weak place in the harness of the English Congregational churches.'[42]

Even Benjamin Nightingale would have agreed with this, though he was thoroughly suspicious of anything which would threaten the autonomy of the local church:

> What, now, is the distinctive Principle of Congregationalism?...The answer may be given in one word - Autonomousness. The Congregational idea of a Church is that of a company of persons redeemed by Jesus Christ, voluntarily entering into Fellowship, and because of the presence of Christ in their gatherings self governed. Within recent years the tendency has been to depreciate the latter, and the distinctive Principle of Congregationalism is sought in the supreme

spiritual character of the Church. With
the desire to emphasize this aspect of
the matter one cannot but have the
fullest possible sympathy, the difficulty comes when this is regarded as the
differentiating quality of Congregationalism.[43]

With this position P.T. Forsyth was in
agreement: 'I believe with Dr. Nightingale
that the distinctive thing about Congregationalism is autonomy. It is not spiritually. That
is not distinctive. it belongs to other bodies. It is an invidious claim.'[44] Nightingale
recognised that in taking his stand he was op-
posing such highly regarded historians as
Powicke and Peel, but he was unrepentant. Our
own view is that those on both sides of the
argument asserted too strong a disjunction,
and that it is perfectly possible to hold that
Congregationalism's essence is a spirituality,
a sainthood, which has implicit within it both
autonomy and fellowship. We might even suggest
that Peel was toppling too far away from the
spiritual ideal in asserting the measure of
local autononomy that he also did: 'A Church
of Christians with Christ in the midst can be
moderated by Moderators, counselled by Bishops, guided by ministers, fraternally advised
by other churches, and because it belongs to
the One Church it will benefit by all these;
but it is itself competent to make the final
decision in all matters affecting its faith
and practice.'[45] Too often this last clause
has meant in practice, that it can ignore all
the rest.
During the course of the independency debate some made the practical point that it was
easier for a minister to exist without external fellowship in a large church than in a

small one;[46] and to a critic of the inter-War
Forward Movement who engagingly opined that
the Movement was 'an attempt to force connec-
tionalism down our throats behind our backs,'
Arthur Pringle replied that 'our headquarters,
the Moderators, and all the great proposals
sponsored by the Forward Movement are the
healthy and inevitable expression of true
Independency, and not its negation.'[47] Despite
this Dr. Micklem could, as late as 1943, diag-
nose Congregationalism's ailment thus: 'We
have asserted the independence of the local
congregation as the sole Congregational principle; therefore, we have missed and over-
looked a vital part of our religious inheri-
tance, and having no religious or theological
principle to guide our denominational development in the relation of churches to each other
we have been thrown back upon mere expediency.'[48] That this was too sweeping a judgment
will become plain if, having now treated of
sainthood and autonomy in our period we turn
more systematically to those who positively
advocated organised inter-church fellowship.

Those who sought to organise the fellowship
of churches did not have an easy passage. The
fears which had overtaken the minds of some
lingered on, and on occasion Presbyterianism
was held up as an example of a polity to be
shunned: 'Congregationalism and primitive
Christianity, place all church power in the
hands of the particular congregations of
believers in their popular capacity. Under
Presbyterianism the great body of the laity
are almost as utterly divested of all power
whatever, as they would be under the Czar of
all the Russias.'[49] The fact that by 1846 a
mere one hundred and seventy-three members
gathered for the Annual Assembly of the Congregational Union suggests that the suspicions

to which we draw attention were fairly widespread. Some independent souls, such as the
doughty William Jay of Bath, sat relatively
loosely to church polity, and would, if anything, have gone further than most in the
direction of Presbyterianism:

> Perhaps, had I been left to choose, in-
> stead of being led by circumstances, I
> should have preferred Presbyterianism,
> as to church order and regimen. But the
> truth is, I never deeply studied the
> theories of ecclesiastical government...
> By the providence of God, I was trained
> among the Independents, and with them I
> remained. I agreed not in every iota of
> their system, but I approved of it in
> the main...But could it not be relieved
> of a little of its democracy, and of its
> great dependence on individual suffrage?
> Or would a change here...introduce an
> agency, more exceptionable and liable to
> abuse?[50]

Algernon Wells, who became Secretary of the
Union (1837-50) was none too enamoured of
moves towards association at first. Said
Thomas Binney at Wells's funeral, 'When the
Congregational Union was first projected, he
did not feel quite sure that it was allowable
or safe!'[51] And when Wells did come to justify
the Union he denied that it had any claims to
scriptural authority; it was simply 'a voluntary and human expedient.'

The argument from expediency was that most
frequently employed by those who advocated the
Union. The work to be done was vast; churches
could not begin to tackle it unaided or in
idolation; accordingly, they must organise for
mission and service. After all, declared John

Kelly at the 1850 Assembly, 'A promiscuous rabble accomplish nothing;' and he pleaded with those who had remained thus far aloof from the Union to come in.[52] A similar note was struck in the following year by Dr. John Harris: 'If, indeed, our church-independence and our denominational unon were two things so inherently hostile that they could not co-exist, I should certainly sacrifice the latter; feeling, however, that the painful necessity considerably detracted from the value of the former. But the truth is, the combination of the two not only involves no compromise, each supposes the other, and is unsatisfied and incomplete without it.' He went so far as to claim that 'Congregational churches alone are capable of true denominational union. In other sections of the church there may be a union of church officers, but not a union of churches.'[53]

When Dr. Halley came to review the first twenty-five years of the Union's life he found much to be thankful for: 'To me it seems of great importance to give demonstration to the whole world, that we have a deliberative Assembly (where the decision has not a particle of authority over any man on earth) with as much solicitude and carefulness as if we could enforce our decison with all the authority of a synod, a conference, or an episcopal convocation.'[54] J.G. Miall saw no reason to be complacent, however; for although those in the Union realise 'in how extensive a sense we belong together...it cannot yet be said of us that we present the aspect of a strong well-marshalled body, ready to defend our positions against all comers, and to take a vigorous action upon what concerns the interests of our Dissenting churches.'[55] Miall's Address was listened to with 'marked attention, and many

passages of it called forth general and earnest cheering.'[56] Among those influenced by
Miall's approach was J.A. Macfadyen, who became an ardent supporter of organised Congregationalism, and who 'preferred the historic
term "consociations" to the modern term "associations" of churches, because it suggested
that churches were in fellowship with each
other essentially, and not merely by voluntary
agreement.'[57]

Unions came increasingly to be defended.
Ralph Wardlaw showed that there was nothing in
Congregational history to condemn them, since
the obligation of fellowship and the need of
mutual advice and exhortation had ever been
recognised by Congregationalists.[58] Others
adverted to the missionary challenge as requiring organisation for its lively accep-
tance; and a few were persuaded that apart
from organisation, Congregationalism would
disappear. Surely few extolled the Assembly
itself as lyrically as did W. Cuthbertson:
'Nay, what means this Congregational Union of
England and Wales? Sweeter than the May blos-
som is it to look into the face of a loved
comrade in arms after the separation of a
dreary winter and a cold snowy spring.'[59]
Alfred Rowland sought to strike the balance:
'Although we Congregationalists do not believe
in any elaborate ecclesiastical organisation,
divinely ordained and historically continuous,
outside which there is no acceptable work or
worship, we believe as little in unorganised
Christianity;'[60] and it is interesting to note
the earliest Congregational justification we
have found of this position in terms of the
increasingly widespread, if largely Anglican,
incarnational-Alexandrian theology: 'We regard
Christian churches as institutions inspired by
Christ,who in them becomes again incarnate...[61]

Many, of course, would have endorsed Dr.
Henry Allon's proviso that 'So long as the
Union maintains its character as a voluntary
confederation for fellowship and work of independent Churches, it is both unimpeachable and
invaluable;'[62] and doubtless not a few denominational officials in Allon's day and since
have said 'Amen' to his realisation that there
are 'locomotive and practical difficulties in
the practical maintenance of fellowship and
co-operation which, in the absence of cumpul-
sory law or denominational bond, are often
preventive.'[63] The Congregational Union was as
yet far from thinking of itself as a churchly
body.

With the passage of time some became increasingly concerned lest the energies of the
Union should be so dissipated as to render its
witness ineffective. That Joseph Parker was of
such a mind is clear from his 1876 Assembly
Address: 'What an amazing amount of so-called
'business' we have to do! We have to desestab-
lish the Church, modernize the Universities,
rectify the policy of School Boards, clear the
way to burial-grounds, subsidize magazines,
sell hymn-books, play the hose upon Convocation, and generally give everybody to understand that if we have not yet assailed or
defended them, it is not for want of will, but
merely for want of time.'[64] On the general
question of Union Parker's position was ambiv-
alent, not to say inconsistent. In his Autobiography (1903) he presents himself as an oppo-
nent of organised Congregationalism; yet in
his Assembly Address of 1901 he advocated the
creation of 'The United Congregational
Church,' and said, 'Instead of having a partially or loosely organised Congregationalism
I wish to take part in the creation and full
equipment of an institution to be known and

developed as the United Congregational Church.'[65] Such a Church would 'Beyond all doubt' preserve 'the central principle of Congregationalism which finds expression in the individual Church.'[66] Parker's detailed proposals were not accepted en bloc, but there can be no doubt that he encouraged the Union in the direction of improved sustentation arrangements, or that he created a climate favourable to the revision of the Union Constitution in 1904 in these terms:

1. Certain powers and duties belong to the individual Church in self-government under the Headship of the Lord Jesus Christ, due regard being had to the interests of other Churches of our own and other denominations. For example: The reception and dismissal of members; the discipline necessary to preserve purity of communion; the election of pastor and deacons; the order of worship; financial arrangements; and all that concerns the internal administration of the Church.

2. Certain duties and responsibilities concern Congregational Churches as a whole, and these can be most effectively fulfilled by a union of Churches. For example: Congregational Church exension, and the promotion of missionary work at home and abroad...

It is noteworthy that for the first time there appears a reference to churches of other denominations in section one; and that the ground of the union commended in section two continues to be expediency.

From time to time some rose up to remind their brethren that organisation would not by itself win the day, and that the vitality or otherwise of the spiritual life of the churches was what mattered;[67] Dr. Micklem over-stated the point in lamenting that unlike other denominations, Congregationalism could not act as a body;[68] and Dr. Grieve seems to have had more of the history behind him in contending that 'It is a libel to say that the local churches had no dealings with one another. It is one of the divine paradoxes that separatism and catholicity meet in the Congregational way. We stand for the fullest possible association of the freest possible units.'[69]

In the document produced at the Wellesley Assembly of the International Congregational Council in 1949 we detect a new way of presenting the case for union. The local church meeting is represented as being the model for the wider unions, and this is, clearly, a stage on the way to the articulation of the idea that all the local churches together comprise a churchly body: 'Local Congregational churches have united with other Congregational churches and with other communions for the purpose of wider fellowship and wider service. These wider unions are extensions of the principle of church government and church authority exemplified in the church meeting. It is Christ who rules in His Church; therefore to no individuals or courts is given coercive authority in the Church. Where Congregational churches have entered into union with other churches, it has been upon the principle that wider synods and courts of the church should have the same sort of authority as the church meeting; that is, they should seek to find the will of Christ for his Church by prayer and

discussion, and being led to a common mind
should have the spiritual authority of the
church meeting. It is our fundamental principle that in all the organization of the church
at every level, all authority is spiritual, or
as our fathers put it, ministerial, not legal-
istic, coercive and magisterial.'[70]

It goes without saying that no modern Congregationalist of note has declared that any
one particular organisational shape of the
Church is sacrosanct or incapable of modification. They have joined with one of Congregationalism's most far-sighted theologians in
denying that the Church is primarily an institution whose authenticity can be vouched for
in a legal way;[71] and with one of Congregationalism's most genial 'administrators' in
affirming that 'Immediately an attempt is made
to declare what organization is indispensable
to a true Church the first step is taken to
divide the Church.'[72] Congregationalists have
ever felt more reassured than most when such
words have fallen from the lips of their executive officers!

Having now given general consideration to
sainthood, autonomy and fellowship in our
period, it remains to enter a most important
caveat. Although in the interests of clarity
we are adhering resolutely to our brief of
tracing the Congregational idea of the Church,
it would be false to suggest that external
factors had no bearing upon the way in which
the idea was formulated. In three ways in
particular the general theologico-religious
climate influenced Congregational thought.

First, Anglo-Catholicism, with its high
emphasis, prompted some Congregationalists to
announce that they also were high Churchmen -
indeed, that they were the true high Churchmen, the genuine Catholics.[73] They reasserted

the catholicity implicit in the Congregational
idea of sainthood, maintaining that all whom
Christ had called to himself were one in him;
and making it abundantly plain that <u>their</u> understanding of high Churchmanship was far re-
moved from sacerdotalism. Not only does Congregationalism not set up a priestly caste, it
'represses the domineering power of the
priesthood.'[74] Dr. Charles Berry, a self-
styled high Church Congregationalist, asked
what such a title meant: 'no one will suspect
it of the least taint of sacerdotalism. It is
the affirmation of the Church, of the Church's
privileges, powers, and duties, as against the
individualist on the one hand, who thinks he
can complete his spiritual culture and fulfil
his duty to Christ and humanity without coming
into associated fellowship, and on the other
hand as against the priests, who have arro-
gated to themselves the functions and even the
very name of the Church, and have insinuated
themselves into dominion where they were under
debt of service.'[75]

Dr. Macfadyen made out a similar case in
even greater detail:

> What the Romanist claims for his Church,
> we claim for our Churches. We accept his
> affirmations, only we apply them differ-
> ently. The Romanist cannot take higher
> ground than we do. The Congregationalist
> does not so much oppose as supersede Ro-
> manism. Does the Romanist maintain that
> grace resides in the Pope, and that the
> Church - meaning by that the clergy - is
> the conduit of that grace? We substitu-
> te Christ for the Pope, and say the same
> thing of the men whom He has made kings
> and priests unto God...Does the Romanist
> claim supernatural grace for the sacra-

> ments and worship of his Church? So do
> we for the sacraments and worship of our
> Churches...Does the Romanist plead that
> the Head of His Church has a right to
> universal obedience? We make the same
> claim for the Head of our Churches...
> Thus the Romanist and the Congregation-
> alist stand at the extreme points of the
> curve...A great conflict is impending...
> Against us Popery wields the hilt with-
> out the sword. [76]

'Congregationalism,' declared P.T. Forsyth,
'is High Church or nothing;' [77] and as for
catholicism, when Henry Allon argues that
'Because we are Congregationalists we are of
necessity Catholics. For more than this we do
not care to contend,' [78] we wonder for what
more Congregationalists <u>could</u> contend.

It was this emphasis upon the catholicity
of sainthood which was to facilitate Congregational participation in the modern ecumenical
movement. As early as the first meeting of the
International Congregational Council (1891),
we are informed that 'Our polity is the only
one under heaven, or which even heaven can
produce, ample enough and free enough, and fit
enough to furnish union for the denominations.' [79] Such a remark could, however - in
the late nineteenth century, at least - be
taken in an idealistic sense. Certainly that
<u>earthed</u> sainthood for which Congregationalists
at their best had ever contended was never
more imperilled than when Fairbairn, at this
point more influenced by Hegel than by
scripture, constantly reiterated his view that
the Church 'is not material, but spiritual.' [80]
In Congregationalism it is both. The tradit-
onal balance was reasserted at Wellesley in
1949: 'We acknowledge Christ to be the sole

Head of the Church. We believe that where He
is present among His people there is all that
is essential to a Church. Thus each community
of believers is the Catholic Church in essence
and is empowered by Christ to govern its own
life under the guidance of His Spirit.'[81]

The second nineteenth century influence to
which we should advert is the rise of modern
biblical criticism. This is not the place to
recount the story in detail,[82] but we must
note the fact that the new approach to scripture necessitated a fresh consideration of the
basis of Congregational polity. The seventeenth century fathers had regarded the Bible
as prescribing a (even one only) political
pattern for the Church. This pattern was to
abide for all time.[83] By the early years of
the nineteenth century some were found modi-
fying this position. If Walter Wilson went
further than most in saying in 1814 that 'no
form of ecclesiastical polity now in being has
any legitimate claim to a divine right; neither are the institutions of the apostolical
Church so clearly defined in every particular
as to prevent the possibility of mistake,'[84]
many were beginning to see that while Congregationalism might be said to be the polity
most in harmony with scripture, its every detail was not prescribed therein. 'I cannot,'
said Dr. Collyer, 'but consider Congregational
churches most consonant with constitution of
primitive churches: and their modes of worship
as best according with scriptural simplicity
and as most conducive to spirituality.'[85] John
Alexander could with some justice declare from
the Chair of the Union in 1853 that 'The order
and polity of our churches have been derived
from the New Testament,'[86] but William Jay was
quicker than many to realise that others could
say the same: 'I do not think, as I have ex-

pressed myself in one of my lectures, any very
particular form of government is absolutely
laid down in the New Testament. I am not igno-
rant that this will surprise and offend several classes of advocates, all of whom appeal to
the Scriptures, and all of whom find their
peculiar and opposite systems laid down there
clearly and definitely - that is, to themselves. Yet there are not wanting in the New
Testament general principles of church-govern-
ment, which will admit, without subverting
them, of considerable modifyings, in their ap-
plication, according to times, places, and
circumstances.'[87]

But Ralph Wardlaw and H.M. Dexter were unequivocal in their testimomy that Congregationalism was the best polity;[88] and soon
Henry Allon and others were found producing
such Anglicans as Whately, Lightfoot, Stanley
and Hatch out of their advocate's hats: each
of these divines had affirmed the congregational nature of the early church.[89] All of
which added strength to Dr. Grieve's case: 'Do
not...be misled by any assertion that all
derive from and broke away from Episcopacy.
Both it and Presbyterianism are offshoots from
us, and from the New Testament Church. The
Early Church Universal was a Congregational
type.'[90]

It is interesting to note, once again, the
influence of nineteenth century idealism upon
the way in which some of our authors express
themselves. Thus, Dale points out that 'Most
modern Congregationalists would decline to
rest the argument for Congregationalism on
precedents recorded in the Acts of the Apostles or on texts quoted from the Epistles. We
prefer to find the laws of ecclesiastical
polity in the laws of spiritual life, in the
objects for which Christian churches exist, in

the central principles of the teaching of
Christ.'[91]   But when Dr. Powicke goes even
further and deems the character of Christianity to be 'a Gospel of the spirit,'[92] it is
difficult to avoid the feeling that we are in
the presence of one desparately trying to
shield the faith from hostile, naturalistic
biblical criticism. The threat to the idea of
the <u>visibility</u> of the saints is clear. No
doubt this threat was in Dr. Stoughton's mind
when he lamented the way in which the scriptural authority for Congregationalism had come
to be forsaken in favour of arguments from
rationality and expediency. For their part the
fathers knew where they stood: 'They stood not
on quickstands, at the mercy of changing cur-
rents, but <u>on a rock</u>. It is a great loss, I am
convinced, to leave that solid ground.'[93]

Thirdly, the spirit of nineteenth-century
individualism communicated itself to the Congregationalism with two results important for
our theme. Some came to construe Independency
individualistically, and to sit loose to
church order; others, inspired by the same
spirit, sat loose to doctrine. Some, truth to
tell, sat loose to both; but it will conduce
to clarity if we treat of order and doctrine
in turn. We may have in review the question,
'Do <u>any</u> two or three gathered in Christ's name
constitute a <u>church</u>'?

In relation to church order F.J. Powicke
gave an affirmative answer to this question.
Addressing the Cheshire Union in 1898 he
denied that ministry, sacraments and organization were essential to the Church, and argued
that 'even two or three, with Christ among
them, are a complete Church.'[94] Dale had earlier made the same point,[95] and two papers
delivered at the 1920 International Congregational Council were to reaffirm it.[96] None of

the critics of this view wished to deny the
particularity of the church, but they wished
to emphasise the nature of the church as ordered. Dr. Barrett, for example, quoted
Butler, 'perhaps the deepest thinker the
English nation has ever produced,' as saying,
'I have known many cases in which the form of
religion has existed without the spirit; I
have never known any where the spirit has existed without the form.'[97]

Those who came in increasing numbers to
maintain both the visibility and the orderliness of the saints jumped backwards over the
early years of their own century, shunned the
individualistic nineteenth century, exalted
John Owen and others, and adopted the term
'Genevan' as descriptive of their stance
(thereby playing down the anabaptist inheri-
tance which Forsyth, to whom they were otherwise much indebted, never forgot). Dr.Micklem,
a leading Genevan, who considerably influenced
the churchmanship of many students of
Mansfield College, Oxford, of which he was
Principal, replied to Albert Peel's Inevitable
Congregationalism (1937), and advanced the
view that while a gathered company of two or
three believers are representative of the
Church, they do not comprise a Church. After
all, he said, two or three believing Anglicans
do not comprise a Congregational church. A
Congregational church is 'a body of Christian
believers organised according to a polity
derived from the New Testament;' hence, 'Gene-
van churchmanship, which we represent, is in
many ways a revival of early Christianity.'[98]
Dr. A.J.B. Higgins concurred,[99] as did Dr.
John Whale and those who formed the Church
Order Group (1946). Few have expounded the
Genevan ideal as felicitously as Dr. Daniel
Jenkins:

It should be carefully noted...that what constitutes a congregation as an independent church is not the fact that it gathers together but the fact that it possesses the ordinance of Christ for His Church. That is to say, it is the marks of Christ which are the marks of the Church, and not any generalized spirit of religious interest or any particular form of organization. Congregationalism takes very seriously the definition of classical Calvinism that wherever the Word is faithfully preached and the Sacraments administered according to Christ's appointment, there the Church is to be found. It differs from other Reformed churches in this respect only in the extent to which it follows out the implications of this definition in relation to the local church's common life.[100]

Bernard Manning teased some with his language, and consoled others with his inference when he said that 'The visible organised local church is for us the earthen vessel which carries the real presence of the Saviour. From this there has always followed among us a vigorous conscious churchmanship which refuses to acknowledge any superior or equal power on earth, which asserts its complete right to self-government and self- discipline.'[101]

By the time Dr. Huxtable could say that the Church 'must have a sociological as well as a spiritual manifestation,'[102] the debate had entered upon a further phase; for the point at issue now was not the ordering of the local church, but the ordering of the total Congregational community as a churchly body. To this theme we shall return in our final chapter.

The reference to the sacraments in our quotation from Dr. Jenkins prompts a brief digression. The place of the Lord's Supper in worship came increasingly to occupy the attention of 'Genevan' Congregationalists. The Supper, they declared, must not be regarded as an optional extra for the particularly devout, which takes place at the close of the 'first' service. Rather, in the full diet of worship, Word and Sacraments belong together. But this degree of liturgical orderliness having been achieved, the question was raised, implicitly if not always in practice, Who may come to the Table? There can be no doubt that partly under a misinterpretation of John Wesley's view that the Supper could be a converting ordinance, and partly as a consequence of nineteenth-century individualism, there had been a gradual, though not a universal, movement from the position that members of the local church alone lay partake of the sacrament in their church; through the position that commended members of other churches might partake of the sacrament in local Congregational churches; to the position that since the Table is the Lord's, all who love him may come, whether or not they are members of the Church. In those churches which took this final step, the traditional ideas of sainthood and catholicity had become seriously weakened. Whereas the Congregational fathers, from Savoy through Watts to Dale, would have said that to love the Lord is to be of his people - that is, it is to be an enrolled saint - it was now being implied if not stated that a person could share in the privileges of the saints without being an enrolled saint. This in turn could not but undermine older notions of church discipline; for the sanction of suspension from communion could hardly be brought against

the saints if the Supper were open to the
'world' with no questions asked.

In doctrinal terms our question is 'May any
two or three constitute a Congregational
church no matter what they believe?' Point was
given to the question by the memory that the
old Presbyterian had, for the most part, become Unitarian, the Westminster Confession
notwithstanding; by the reductionism of those
who jumped upon the 'not creed, but life' band
waggon; and by such eccentrics as Dr. W.E.
Orchard who, far from being a reductionist,
believed considerably <u>more</u> than his fellow
churchmen and ended in Rome. The answers given
to the question must be seen in relation to
the general Congregational attitude towards
creeds and confessions. This attitude has en-
compassed the following points:

1. That it is not confessional sub-
    scription (any more than it is resi-
    dence in a parish) that makes the
    individual a Christian.
2. That credal subscription shall not
    be a test of membership, because to
    ask for anything other than a pro-
    fession of faith in Christ is of the
    essence of sectarianism.
3. That it is entirely appropriate that
    both local churches and the wider
    fellowship of churches should set
    down the things commonly believed
    among them.
4. That while creeds and confessions
    may bear witness to a commonly held
    faith they neither create nor sus-
    tain it.
5. That creeds and confessions may, un-
    happily, encourage assent to extra-
    scriptural authority on the one hand

and the fossilisation and cerebralisation of faith on the other.

6. That it is by the Holy Spirit and (humanly speaking) by their devotional life that churches are kept true to the faith once delivered to the saints: 'to call it a safeguard is to speak on too mean a level. It is of the essence of our existence.'[103]

Even before the nineteenth-century's wide variety of belief options had come into view Congregationalists were contemplating the question of belief in relation to church membership. As early as 1821 we find attempts to develop a casuistry which will enable the orthodox to deal with the Unitarian - who, as time goes on is ubiquitous in the literature. Thus 'T' contests the view that Unitarians, who lost the truth, are, whatever their polity, Independents; for the Independent peculiarity is that 'their churches are formed of such persons as, it is hoped, are "sanctified in Christ Jesus," and "called to be saints;" and it is to the instrumentality of this part of their system, that the preservation of the truth among them is here attributed. It is well known, however, that the Unitarians do not adopt this important branch of Independency, but even treat it with scorn and derision.'[104] John Alexander was not the only Chairman of the Union to maintain that the Congregational polity 'is adapted to secure a firm adherence to evangelical doctrines. [105] The implication of this as far as 'The External Relations of Congregationalism' were concerned was that while we may not co-operate in worship and effort with those who hold 'discordant opinions, we do not presume to know or to judge their status before the Lord.[106] The American Dr. Charles E. Jefferson drove to the doctrinal heart of the matter: 'The fundamental thing in Congregationalism is a doctrine of God...We are free men in Christ. We are at liberty to build the church along the lines indicated by the Eternal Spirit...so that it shall become more and more an effective instrument in the hands of God...'[107]

But the practical question arises, 'What of the individual who holds Unitarian beliefs and yet asks for membership of a Congregational church?' R.W. Dale faced this question, and on grounds of fellowship, and because of his conviction that men are often better than their beliefs, and that they are more likely to grow in congenial soil, declared that he would accept such a one;[108] and in a letter to Dr. Finlayson he wrote, 'Can a man have faith in Christ - the faith which saves - and yet deny the Divinity of His Person? You say Yes: I say Yes. And I accept the logical result of the position in relation to polity.'[109] At the same time, however, Dale denied that anything less than full-blooded evangelicalism was truly Congregational: 'if any Church received Socinian or Tridentine doctrine, it would cease to be Congregational...not merely because for three centuries Congregationalism has been historically identified with Evangelical theology, but because, with the rejection of that theology, the theory of the Congregational polity would be rejected too.'[110] In the same decade J.A. Macfadyen reminded the Lancashire Union that 'in the common usage of the word, Congregationalism includes the idea of attachment to evangelical theology.'[111]

With the growing impact of theological liberalism some Congregationalists began to be increasingly concerned by the teaching of such men as Francis Wrigley of Salem, Leeds. Typical of his statements are the following: 'Are you wanting to be like Christ?...Are you in earnest about being good?...The basis of membership...is not theological or emotional, but practical.'[112] Elsewhere he said that 'Our strength lies in ourselves, our personal conviction, our personal loyalty, our personal possession of the Spirit of Christ.'[113] Such anthropocentric sentiments as these drew the fire of Dr. D.W. Simon who, however, clearly felt that he was swimming against the tide:

> Last year I had made up my mind to force on a discussion...of the proposed creedlessness of the new Constitution of the Congregational Union, but gave it up partly because I really have not the needed nervous energy...and partly because I feel it is useless. The day is passed. Whether Congregationalism will ever get back to a strong doctrinal position I don't know; but it will take years, and I am not the man to stir - because I am too advanced in reality, and yet too conservative in the view of the majority.[114]

His own conviction was that 'the Christian Gospel is a gospel because it consists of credenda, facts of faith, given objectively, if not in Scripture as a whole, yet in and through the historical Person - Jesus Christ; that from these the Church has always derived its Evangelical witness and experience; that, in this sense, the Congregational Churches have been consistently Evangelical, and have inherited and Evangelical tradition; that, therefore, non-Evangelical Churches or professors, or ministers, or members that claim to

be Congregational are sailing under false
colours.'[115] Simon certainly felt that to
allow a Unitarian to _propagate_ his faith
within a Congregational church on the ground
of the independency of that church, was
'Independency gone mad.'[116]

With respect to liberal thought in general,
Albert Goodrich warned the third assembly of
the International Congregational Council that
as far as that thought was concerned, 'There
is no Christ who outside knocks at the door,
but only a Christ within, sleeping, who, indeed, is but our better self. As idealism
creates the world out of its own ideas, so
modernism creates religion out of its own
soul.'[117] There was even the danger that whole
churches could be adversely affected by theological novelties. P.T. Forsyth recounted how

> An eminent but orthodox and puzzled Con-
> gregationalist layman once said to me
> that if a Church became unanimous in
> rejecting an historic Christ, or an
> apostolic Gospel, in favour of "the
> spirit of Christ," it was difficult to
> see how it could be shown to have ceased
> to be Congregationalist. The answer was
> that it had not ceased to be Congrega-
> tionalist, as the Unitarians have not;
> it had ceased to be a Church. It had, in
> principle, renounced the Holy Spirit of
> the final Word for a spirit of charita-
> ble religiosity...For a Church is not
> made by a certain subjective temper, nor
> by long existence, nor by the will of
> man, nor by the unanimity of wills in a
> vote; but by a positive historic revela-
> tion of ageless Gospel, by a new cre-
> ative act of God, and by the consequent
> presence and life in it of Jesus Christ,

whose cross is the one source of the
Holy Spirit.[118]

The main point here is sufficiently clear,
even if the last clause is more than a little
puzzling. More recently Dr. C.J. Cadoux was
found announcing that neither Unitarians,
Quakers nor Salvationists ought to be barred
from church fellowship. He argued that any
barriers would be equivalent to credal tests,
and that such tests do not in fact keep out of
church fellowship those who ought to be kept
out, but that they do debar many who ought to
be welcomed; that the Holy Spirit is to be
trusted to lead Christ's disciples into all
truth; and that Congregationalism's 'open
door' does not bring disaster on the
Church.[119] Even Dr. Lovell Cocks, who echoed
his revered teacher Forsyth when he said, 'The
Church is the Church God gathers. Its foundation is in His free grace, and its beginning
is in His saving Word,' yet acknowledged that
'men's minds may well lag behind their self-
committal.'[120] But whatever their pastoral
practice in particular cases, the general
consensus of Congregationalists was ever to
give a negative answer to Dr. Dexter's
rhetorical question: Is it, he asked, 'honour-
able for those who deny the distinctive principles of Evangelical religion to seek to get
their alien cuckoo's eggs hatched in our Congregational nest?'[121]

During the period of denominational Congregationalism the body corporate was character-
ized by general loyalty to evangelical truth;
by the conviction that the Congregational
polity was at the very least biblically defen-
sible; by varying degrees of willingness to
allow fellowship to find expression through
organisation - this both nationally, and in-

ternationally through the International Congregational Council[122]; and by the perennial
desire to ensure that such organization should
pose no threat to the proper autonomy of the
local church. All thought that the Church comprises saints, though some thought that their
local gatherings should be more, others less,
formally ordered. The highest of high Church
Congregationalists, however, had no patience
with sacerdotalism. Finally, there were tenta-
tive moves in the direction of the view that
corporate Congregationalism was no mere expedient, but was a clear implication of the Congregational understanding of catholic sainthood, and that it could find its organization-
al expression on the analogy of the local
church meeting.

6. Churchly Congregationalism

It has traditionally been a matter of principle with Congregationalists that there can be no such thing as a Congregational churchly body in the sense of a 'third Church' subsisting between the local church and the Church catholic. Reflecting upon the qualms which were expressed by some when the Congregational Union was first mooted, Dr. Mackennal remarked that 'the Congregationalists of that time were very jealous indeed of the interposition of any body whatever between the individual church and the whole family in heaven and in earth.'[1] Having been formed, the Union had no difficulty at all in publishing tracts which underlined that view: 'Anything - e.g. an ecclesiastical court - or anyone - e.g., a diocesan or other bishop - that can authoritatively interpose, or pronounce and execute a sentence, we hold to be exercising a power contrary to the spirit and the liberty of Christ.'[2] A similar, possibly earlier, tract was even blunter: 'The only organised church Congregationalism owns is a <u>particular church or congregation of believers</u> statedly meeting in <u>one place</u>. A provincial or national church, including many particular churches, and governed by general officers, has no place in the Congregational system.'[3]

No doubt some of this spirit was engendered by the sacerdotalism of the largest churchly

body known to nineteenth-century Congregationalists, and Baldwin Brown spoke for many of
them:

> I dread when I hear about 'the Church'.
> I think of prelates, priests, tithes,
> law-books, sacraments, and spiritual
> persons and orders. When I hear about
> the churches, the little households of
> Christ, my heart is uplifted...We must
> maintain at all hazards the entire inde-
> pendence of the churches of all but
> brotherly guidance and influence. Harden
> into an Independent body, you may look
> larger and stronger, and may make a more
> monotonous order in your house of life.
> But you may write 'Ichabod' on your tem-
> ples; your strength has departed, your
> glory is gone.[4]

But quite apart from what we might call the
environmental and temperamental dissuasives to
the 'third Church' idea, there were the scriptural. Dr. Wardlaw combed the New Testament
and concluded that apart from Acts xix:41,
where the term 'church' is used of a concourse
of people, it means either the whole Israel of
God, or the society of believers in one place.[5] Many agreed, and the spate of Congregational manuals to which the later years of the
nineteenth century gave birth underlined the
point.[6] In an article reprinted in The Congregationalist the American Dr. Eddy wrote that
'While...Congregationalism has always recognised Christian Churches of every denomination, it has never, except in courtesy, given
that name to the denominations themselves.
None but a novice would ever call the aggre-
gate of our Churches "the Congregational
Church."'[7] Ninety years later there were many

'novices' in English Congregationalism!

In addition to disquiet at the activities of the Anglican churchly body, and to the absence of the term 'church' used in the denominational sense from the New Testament, there was the feeling that to apply the term to the body corporate would be a mark of sectarianism; it would subvert that very catholicity of Congregationalism which, to some, was among its greatest attractions. In this connection Dr. Mackennal's testimony is instructive: 'In early years I was an extreme Independent, and I was so in the interest of Catholicity. I loved to think that there was nothing between the Local Church and the Church Universal, - the fellowship in heaven and on earth. I refused, on the platform of the Congregational Union, the name <u>body</u> to the Congregational denomination: "There is one body - the body is of Christ." I also dreaded the appeal to the <u>esprit de corps</u>, lest zeal for a denominational unity should take the place of devotion to the things of the spirit.'[8] Dr. Hannay was able to calm his fears to a great extent.

Others were not so easily persuaded, however. Of Joseph Parker's scheme for a United Congregational Church Dr. A.M. Fairbairn wrote,

> I respect the scheme and its authors too much to be willing to accept, because of their good intentions, what would be to me an historical absurdity, and the surrender of all that was most Catholic, most characteristic and most true in the conception of the Church. But happily the use of this name has nothing to do with the ideal it has been used to denote and with its intrinsic quality. It is a scheme of brotherhood, of mutual help, of federation for high ends, but

is is not a scheme for the incorporation
of single independent societies into a
sole organisation which could not be and
yet spare their independency. Why then
use a term which expresses this, and
which, as so used, has been protested
against, for good and sufficient reasons, by all the men who have understood
and believed in the Congregational ideal
ever since that ideal became a reality.[9]

Just before the outbreak of the Second
World War J.S. Griffith was found making the
same point: 'The glory of our Congregationalism is that we refuse to make the Church of
our Lord a theological sect...Elsewhere, to
some degree, greater or less in each case,
fellowship with the Church Universal is prohibited or made difficult: and to join such a
Church, even in the name of union or re-union,
would be to cut myself off, just to that degree, from the Church Universal...'[10] Dr. C.J.
Cadoux agreed, delighting to remind his readers that 'Congregationalist' is the Latin
equivalent for the partially Greek 'church-
man,' and noting that the denominational offices at Memorial Hall obscured 'for many of
our own members - and still more for those
outside our ranks - the essential catholicity
of our position.'[11] That there is, properly
speaking, 'no such thing as "the Congregational Church" in a denominational sense'[12] was
Cadoux's considered opinion. The Report of the
Special Committee appointed by the Executive
Committee of the Lancashire Congregational
Union to consider the Joint Conference Report
on Proposals for Union between the Congregational churches of England and Wales and the
Presbyterian Church of England concurred: 'We
do not regard the designation "Church" as

rightly applied to Unions of churches or denominations.'[13]

Even the 'Genevan' Congregationalist Dr.
Micklem accepted the traditional Congregationalist reading of the New Testament evidence,
whilst not fearing the denominational use of
'Church' if the quality of the corporate life
demanded it.[14] Dr. Nuttall was not so san-
guine. With reference to the Joint Conference
Report he said that 'The Report is in terms of
a "United Church." There are still Congregationalists who, for spiritual reasons, could
not accept anything between the Church universal and the local Churches, by membership of
which they are members of the Church Universal, as itself a Church.'[15] More recently
still Dr. Erik Routley argued against the use
of the term 'Church' in the denominational
sense, not because the usage would impede Congregationalism's catholic claim, but as an
'admission that as a body we lack that conti-
nuity which is the mark of the church universal.'[16]

But nothing could suppress the feeling
among Congregationalists that the sense of
belonging together which the Union had fos-
tered had outgrown the rationale of it given
in the 1831 Constitution. Were Congregationalists not, in fact, behaving like a Church?
In the Introduction to his abridgement of
Owen's The True Nature of a Gospel Church Dr.
Huxtable said that 'It is well that Congregational churches should be related to each other; but it would be even better if they understood how they are related, if they could see
that their relatedness is rooted in something
deeper than expediency, and if they could realise that the theology of the Church Meeting
is applicable to union assemblies.'[17] Dr.
Jenkins supplemented this view by reference to

the need to have a Union adequately adapted to
its role: 'It is not merely permissible but
essential that an organ of the communion of
the churches with each other, which in the nature of the case becomes a form of the Church,
should receive the powers necessary for the
effective fulfilment of its function.'[18] The
introduction of Provincial Moderators in 1919,
and the inauguration of the Home Churches Fund
in 1947 were among the factors adverted to in
support of the contention that Congregationalists had become something more than a loose
confederation of individual churches: they
were behaving corporately in a churchly way,
and it was time that theory caught up with
practice.[19] The preamble to the Constitution
of the Congregational Union of England and
Wales was amended in 1957 and 1958 in such a
way as formally to associate the wider fellowship of churches with the local church on the
occasion of ordination services. (In practice
such association had been all but universal).

In 1958, under the leadership of its then
Secretary, Howard Stanley, the Congregational
Union commited itself to a review of its life
and witness under the general heading of 'The
Next Ten Years.' A number of Commissions was
set up, Commission I being charged with the
responsibility of examining the nature of the
Church; the nature of episcope; and the relations of the churches to each other, to the
Union, and to other Christian communions. A
lively debate ensued, and it will be some time
before we can see the events of the last
thirty years in their proper historical per-
spective. Suffice it to say that concern was
expressed by those who felt that the constitution of a Congregational Church in England and
Wales would entail too great a departure from
Congregationalism's historic testimony as to

the nature of the Church; and by some conser-
vative evangelicals who felt in addition that
the position of the Bible as the infallibly
inspired Word of God was inadequately safe-
guarded in the proposed new constitution. Both
parties viewed Dr. Caird's exegesis with suspicion, and countered his claim that in the
New Testament 'church' has one main meaning -
'the whole company of God's people' - and 'a
number of derivative ones;' and that, accordingly, 'we need not hesitate to use the word
church to describe the larger fellowship.'[20]
Dr. Huxtable, less ambiguously, granted that
the proposed use of 'Church' 'certainly has no
literal warrant in scripture.'[21]

Some, at first hesitant concerning the formation of a Congregational Church, became satisfied as further clarification of the role of
the local church vis à vis the national body
was offered, and when the Declaration of Faith
(1967 and earlier drafts) made plain the mutual and ministerial nature of the relationship
envisaged.[22] The majority of Congregationalists, however, was persuaded from the outset
that the constitution of the Congregational
Church in England and Wales was eminently
desirable, and their wish was granted in 1966,
when the majority of Congregational churches
entered into a covenant to that end.[23]

Was the Congregational idea of the Church
lost for ever, as a minority of Congregationalists felt? Our own view is that it was not,
but that Congregationalists were nevertheless
in an irregular position. Let us attempt to
make out this case.

Among the bones of contention in the months
preceding the formation of the Congregational
Church was the question, 'Which body has the
final authority - the Assembly or the local
Church Meeting?' The members of the commission

answered this question as follows:

> Neither. The final authority is in
> Christ. The local Church has the res-
> ponsibility of seeking to learn the will
> of Christ on matters relevant to its own
> life, and the Assembly has the responsi-
> bility of seeking to learn the will of
> Christ for the whole fellowship of
> churches. Each in matters belonging to
> its proper sphere rightly claims the
> authority of Christ for decisions sin-
> cerely made in obedience to Him. Each
> should be prepared to learn from the
> other, and may have to admit that it was
> mistaken. Church Meetings, County Execu-
> tives, and national Church Assemblies
> are all liable to err, and have erred.[24]

It would seem that, nomenclature apart,
this is nearer in spirit to most of the seventeenth century fathers than what came to be
called 'granular independency' ever was, and
the final Constitution of the Congregational
Church gave clear voice to the mutuality here
described.[25] So too did the Declaration of
Faith: 'We affirm our Congregational conviction that the wholeness of Christ's universal
Church may be present in local congregations,
as well as in wider associations, where God
gathers people together in constant relationship for worship, for fellowship, for service
and for witness to the world, under the care
of Christ their Lord.'[26]

As to the name 'Congregational Church,' the
Report of Commission I could hardly have been
plainer: 'The churches thus associated have no
wish to appear as a Denomination in distinction from other Denominations, or to weaken
their own sense of ecumenicity; but since it

is not at present possible to gather all
Christians into one Church Order it is necessary that Congregational churches should express in some corporate form their belonging
together which is so plainly a fact of their
experience.'[27] It would seem that so long as
the term 'Church' was used denominationally as
a temporary, irregular, expedient, Congregational catholicity was unimpaired. It is important that those who inherit the Congregational way should emphasize this irregularity
from time to time, lest those of other Christian communions misunderstand their witness
and come to imagine that the usage of 'Church'
to denote a particular denomination is, to
them, normal; and lest they themselves cease
to feel that pain which, given the divided
nature of the Church visible, their usage of
the term in that sense should make them feel.
In a word, they must never forget that it is a
sad thing to be a Church in the denominational
sense; and this notwithstanding the many
blessings which are theirs by reason of their
fellowship in such a Church. The usage of the
term in this sense witnesses to a divided
Christendom. Certainly there is much psychological and theological advantage in being
united because it is right, and not simply
because it is expedient. The ex-Presbyterians
in the United Reformed Church have underlined
this lesson.

There can be little doubt that the formation of the Congregational Church in England
and Wales facilitated conversations with the
English Presbyterians, which had been conducted intermittently since 1932.[28] (Some of
the more suspicious Congregationalists declared that wider union was the covert objective of the members of Commission I. We may,
however, trust the integrity of those who

denied this, and who said that whatever were
to happen on the wider ecclesiastical front,
the constitution of the Congregational Church
was right in itself). As a result of what
became the final round of negotiations, the
United Reformed Church was born in 1972.

Is it a proper question to ask what has
become of the Congregational way within the
United Reformed Church? In a sense it is not.
The objective was the creation, under God, of
a new Church which should be true to the Bible
and not opposed to the main thrusts of the
traditions from which its members came. Neither erstwhile Congregationalists nor erstwhile
Presbyterians ought to be eager to play 'hunt
the ecclesiologies' by perusing the Scheme of
Union with a view to showing that 'This was
ours, this was theirs.' On the other hand, if
it be true that God gives to all his people
gifts which are for the good of all, then
those whose humbly offered gifts are accepted
by their fellows ought to be able to see
traces of them in the new context. Let us then
inquire what has become of the Congregational
way in the United Reformed Church, and let us
understand this question first ecclesiologically and then, as an implication of this
understanding, pastorally.

The first clause of the Basis of Union
makes it plain that the Church is the calling
of God. The second and sixteenth affirm (albeit not in these words) that the Church comprises saints: its members are Christ's re-
deemed people; the third declares that the
Church is catholic; the fourth makes clear
that its apostolicity is in the gospel, and
(by implication) is not of the sacerdotal
kind.[29] None of this is out of accord with the
Congregational idea of the Church; and John
Robinson would have been quite at home with

the sixth clause: 'Christ's mercy in continuing his call to the Church in all its failure and weakness has taught the Church that its life must ever be renewed and reformed according to the Scriptures, under the guidance of the Holy Spirit.' Here is that 'founded freedom' which Congregationalism prized so highly. Sainthood and catholicity are there; so too is orderliness. The church is an ordered society (and at this point former Congregationalists have been challenged by the Presbyterian understanding of the eldership), but at its heart there remains the <u>church</u> meeting. But all is now set within a fresh and determined context of corporate <u>episcope</u>, whose excitements and challenges will occupy the new Church for some years to come. (No doubt if all else failed the General Assembly could suspend or even expel a church from fellowship, but it could not deny its claim to be a church, however wayward).

So much for the theory; now concerning the practice. Can it be said that the United Reformed Church is as faithful to its principles as even it might be? Saints are priviledged people, and there is no privilege without responsibility. This is one side of the coin. <u>Are</u> church meetings always concerned earnestly and urgently to seek the mind of Christ; to come to that unanimity in him which is his will? Are Synods and Districts never at the mercy of manipulative 'platform' politicians? The other side of the coin concerns the possibility that the privileges of the saints may be squantered. Are 'all comers' welcome to join the church? Are they adequately taught the faith into which they come? Would enquiries into the godliness or otherwise of a prospective member's 'walk' be regarded as quaint - or even 'none of our business'? Ought the only practi-

cal difference between a member and a non-
member be that the latter may not vote at
church meeting? Certainly this would be the
conclusion drawn by an uninstructed observer
of the life of some local churches. Small wonder, then, that if the church meeting is of
the duller sort, some will eschew it - and
with it membership altogether. Is the sacrament of Baptism in practice reserved for those
infants whose parents are within the covenant
- as the last utterance of the Congregational
Union on the subject affirmed that it ought
'normally' to be?[30] Or do baptisms take place
on grounds of 'evangelical opportunity' after
one or two discussions with non-enrolled parents, and in the hope that everything will
work out happily? Ought the objective to be to
instruct, pastor, and receive such parents
into membership first? Does this frequently
happen? Again, is the Lord's Supper a Sacrament of the church, that is, of the saints? Is
it intended to be? Or is Wesley's view that
the Supper may be a converting ordinance
wrongly taken to mean that by itself it can
convert sinners (as distinct from rousing
slumbering saints)? Or do 'politeness' and
lack of curiosity prevail? The United Reformed
Church has the form of sainthood. Does it express in practice the substance of it - and
can it do so until it examines afresh the concept of ecclesiastical discipline which, no
doubt, some of our fathers enjoyed too much,
but which is the inseparable accompaniment of
orderly sainthood? It goes without saying that
no new legalism is here advocated! Rather, we
have in mind that gospel discipline which ever
challenges the saints to mission and service,
and equips them for this; and which, in rarer
cases requires the saints to stand for the
gospel over against those who seem to deny it

- though always with the objective, and in the hope, that estranged parties will be reconciled.

In fairness to the United Reformed Church we recall that, as we have seen, the idea of sainthood had been diluted long before 1972. The challenge of church membership was not always pitched very high; the Lord's Supper was frequently opened to all comers, as if 'loving the Lord' did not imply 'being of his people;' church discipline had in some quarters degenerated into spasmodic, rather embarrassed attempts to 'prune the church roll;' and it could not honestly be said that all Congregationalists shared Dale's delight in attending the Church Meeting. Above all, the erosion of Calvinism and the inroads made by a genial, often uncritically-accepted universalism - not to mention the increasing suspicion in many quarters of anything smacking of elitism - had gnawed away at the foundation-plank of Congregational ecclesiology: the idea of the <u>specialness</u> (i.e. 'peculiarity') of the saints. More recently the reluctance to talk in terms of specialness has been underlined in the eyes of many by the obligation to work for harmony in what is now a pluralist society. It is our conviction that a serious investigation of the disciplinary implications of the issues raised in this paragraph is an urgent requirement, not least in the interest of those local churches, sited in relatively isolated locations (rural or urban), which are expected by the world around them to function as <u>quasi</u> parish churches, and to make available a number of services almost on demand.[31]

In the seventeenth century the Presbyterian Robert Baillie complained that Congregationalism 'is become a uniting principle.'[32] At

its best it has ever been thus, and the principle is at least as old as <u>Savoy</u>. In this
connection the United Reformed Church will
best serve the ecumenical cause by insisting
that Christian unity must be unity in the
gospel; by asserting that membership of the
Church is the gift of God'grace, and that all
whom he calls are of that company; and by op-
posing all versions of the Galatian heresy,
which would circumscribe the gospel by introducing 'new circumcisions.' It was John Howe,
in whom, conveniently enough, Presbyterianism
and Congregationalism were mixed, who declared
that 'Without all controversy the main inlet
of all the distractions, confusions, and divi-
sions of the Christian world, hath been by
adding other conditions of church communion
than Christ hath done.'[33] New circumcisions
are the badge of sectarianism and the denial
of freedom under the gospel. <u>De facto</u> secta-
ries the members of the United Reformed Church
may, sadly, be. But let them beware lest they
become sectarian on principle - ironically, in
the cause of ecumenicity. 'Those,' wrote A.M.
Fairbairn 'who believe that the Church of God
is as broad and as free as the mercy of God,
may well be forgiven if they speak plainly and
frankly about any and every attempt to bind it
to a provincial polity, and to make it seem
less large and less gracious than the action
of God in history has proved it to be.'[34]

Visible sainthood, orderliness and catholicity are marks of the United Reformed understanding of the nature of the Church, as they
are of traditional Congregationalism. May
those who inherit the tradition be as willing
to criticise and to receive as they are to
defend and to share.

Notes

Abbreviations

CHST: Congregational Historical Society
      Transactions
CQ : The Congregational Quarterly
CYB : The Congregational Year Book
PICC: Proceedings of the International
      Congregational Council
CUEW: Congregational Union of England
      and Wales

CHAPTER ONE

1. Art. 'Congregationalism,' The Oxford Dictionary of the Christian Church, ed. F.L. Cross and E.A. Livingstone, London: OUP 2nd edn. 1974, p.332.

2. A.M. Fairbairn, Studies in Religion and Theology, New York: Macmillan 1910,p.111. Cf. this from an internationally-minded Congregationalist: 'The shape of Congregationalism, even its essential shape, is not its essence. Congregationalism did not begin as a kind of church government. When it did take a churchly shape it was to find the way whereby believing Chris-

tians might in fellowship associate for the worship of God, the proclamation of the Gospel, and the Christian way of life.' R.F.G. Calder, 'Congregationalism: A Long View,' CHST XIX 1961, p.66.

3. Robert Mackintosh, 'The Genius of Congregationalism,' in Essays Congregational and Catholic, ed. A. Peel, London: CUEW (1931), p.122. Mackingtosh was a convert - or, as he said, a 'refugee' - to Congregationalism from the Free Church of Scotland. See A.P.F. Sell, Robert Mackintosh: Theologian of Integrity, Bern: Peter Lang 1977.

4. P.T. Forsyth, Faith, Freedom and the Future (1912), London: Independent Press 1955, pp. 290, 336, 347.

5. Matt. xviii: 20.

6. See P.T. Forsyth, op.cit., for the classic statement of this view.

7. The Epistle of St. Ignatius to the Smyrnaens. in The Apostolic Fathers II, London: Farran n.d., p.111.

8. Tertullian, 'On Fasting,' Works, Ante-Nicene Christian Library, ed. Alexander Roberts and James Donaldson, Edinburgh: T.& T. Clark 1870, III, p.147.

9. Cf. Benjamin Nightingale, Congregationalism Reexamined, London: CUEW 1918. pp. 58-9.

10. For whom see R.W. Cleaves, The Story of the Federation; Congregationalism 1960-

_1976_, Swansea: John Penry Press 1977.

11. So Dr. Alonzo Quint in connection with
     the 1865 statement of polity produced by
     American Congregationalists. See G.G.
     Atkins and F.L. Fagley, _History of Amer-
     ican Congregationalism_, Boston: The
     Pilgrim Press 1942, p.291.

12. See Zwingli, _Commentarius de vera et
     falsa Religione_, 1525, II pp.232-3; cf.
     the _Second Helvetic Confession_, 1566,
     chap.XXX.

13. See Calvin, _Institutes_ IV xii; cf. the
     Ecclesiastical Ordinances, 1536.

14. For which see Richard Hooker, _Treatise on
     the Laws of Ecclesiastical Polity_, 1594
     ff; Thomas Cartwright, _Cartwrightiana_,
     ed. A. Peel and Leland H. Carlson,
     London: Allen & Unwin 1951.

CHAPTER TWO

1. _II Cor_. vi:17.

2. _Matt_. xviii:20

3. H.M. Dexter, _The Congregationalism of the
    Last Three Hundred Years as Seen in its
    Literature_, New York: Harper 1880, p.115.

4. _The Trewe Markes of Christes Churche_,
    quoted by Champlin Burrage, _The Early
    English Dissenters_, Cambridge:CUP, 1912,
    II, p.13.
    We modernise spelling in our quotations,
    but retain the original spelling in the

titles of works.

5. Cf. e.g. the Catechism (1581) of the converted Dominican John Craig, in which the marks of the Church are said to be 'The Word, the Sacraments, and Discipline rightly used.' See The School of Faith, trans. and ed. T.F. Torrance, London: James Clarke 1959, p.160.

6. H.M. Dexter, op.cit., p. 115 n.

7. C. Burrage, op.cit., pp.13-14. When, twenty years later, Whitgift urged against the Presbyterian Cartwright that it was 'impossible to permit the churches to elect their own pastors, for the churches were composed of hypocrites, dissemblers, drunkards, whoremongers, and the like,' he was giving the case to the separatists.

8. See J. Robinson, Works, ed. R. Ashton, 1851, III p.428; H. Barrow, A Brief Discoverie of the False Church (1590) in The Writings of Henry Barrow, 1587-1590 ed. Leland H. Carlson, London: Allen & Unwin 1962, pp.287, 306. Barrow observes that those who take the contrary view appeal to Calvin. But Calvin though, despite his 'many errors and ignorances,' 'a faithful and profitable instrument,' was but 'newly escaped out of the smoky furnace of popery;' hence his blind spots. See further, G.F. Nuttall, 'The Early Congregational Conception of the Church,' CHST XIV, 1940-44, pp.197-204.

9. So e.g. R.W. Dale, Essays and Addresses, London: Hodder & Stoughton 1899, p.202;

W.B. Selbie, 'The Religious Principle of Congregationalism,' in <u>Mansfield College Essays</u>, London: Hodder & Stoughton 1909, p.27.

10. W.T. Pennar Davies, 'John Penry,' <u>World Congregationalism</u> IV, no.10, 1962, p.32.

11. See A. Peel, <u>The Noble Army of Congregational Martyrs</u>, London: Independent Press 1948, chs. I and II.

12. 'How [i.e. on what grounds] do they charge us as evil willers to the Queen?' he asks in <u>A Treatise of Reformation without tarying for anie</u> (1582), in <u>The Writings of Robert Harrison and Robert Browne</u>, eds. A.Peel and Leland H. Carlson, London: Allen & Unwin 1953, p.152. Browne's view of the prerogatives of the Prince lends support to Dexter's claim that 'Browne owed nothing to Anabaptist influences.' <u>Op.cit.</u>, p.103. Indeed Browne denies the charge of anabaptism in e.g. <u>A Treatise upon the 23 of Matthewe</u>, in eds. Peel and Carlson, <u>op. cit.</u>, p.215. Nevertheless Browne and the anabaptists held some ecclesiological ideas in common.

13. <u>The Seconde Parte of a Register</u>, ed. A. Peel, Cambridge: CUP 1915, p.158.

14. R. Browne (?), <u>A True and Short Declaration</u> (c.1583) in eds. Peel and Carlson, <u>op.cit.</u>, p.404. We place the word 'deduced' in inverted commas because although many of the Congregational fathers would have regarded themselves as making legitimate deductions from scripture, what they actually did was to draw inferences therefrom; and inference is a

psychological matter involving temperament, selection of material, etc.

15. R.Browne, <u>A Booke which sheweth the life and manners of all true Christians</u> (1582) in eds. Peel and Carlson, <u>op.cit.</u>, p. 226.

16. <u>Ibid</u>., p.253.

17. <u>A Treatise of Reformation</u>, <u>ibid</u>., p.162.

18. <u>A Booke which sheweth</u>, <u>ibid</u>., p.253.

19. <u>Ibid</u>., p.271.

20. A.M. Fairbairn, <u>Studies in Religion and Theology</u>, p.218 n.

21. <u>Ibid</u>., p.213.

22. T.Nash, <u>The Anatomie of Absurditie</u> (1589) ed. R.B. McKerrow, 1904, I, p.22.

23. <u>A Booke which sheweth</u>, <u>op.cit.</u>, p.276.

24. In his counter to Stillingfleet, <u>More Work for the Dean</u>, 1681.

25. So the full title of their <u>Apology</u>.

26. C. Burrage, <u>op.cit.</u>, I, p.28. Cf. G.F. Nuttall, <u>Visible Saints</u>, Oxford: Blackwell 1957, p.8 n.4; <u>An Apologeticall Narration</u>, ed. R.S. Paul, Philadelphia: United Church Press 1963, pp.63-4 and notes.

27. <u>A Brief Discoverie</u>, <u>op.cit.</u>, p.308.

28. For Dr. Carlson's case for this date see

op.cit., pp.173-7.

29. Ibid., p.179.

30. H.M. Dexter, op.cit.,pp.106, 107, 235-9,
     351; W. Walker, The Creeds and Platforms
     of Congregationalism (1893) Boston: Pil-
     grim Press 1960, p.32.

31. H. Barrow, Writings, 1587-1590, p.609;
     cf. A True Confession of the Faith and
     Humble acknowledgment of the Alegeance
     which wee hir Majestie Subjects falsely
     called Brownists doo hould towards God
     and yeild to hir Majectie, 1596. The
     pastor of the 1592 separatist church was
     Francis Johnson; its teacher was Henry
     Ainsworth. From 1609, however, Johnson
     did maintain a Presbyterian position vis
     à vis the eldership. See his A Christian
     Plea, 1617, pp.303-316, and F.J. Powicke,
     Henry Barrowe, London: James Clarke 1900,
     pp. 254 ff., 268 ff.

32. Ibid., pp.608-9.

33. The Writings of John Greenwood, together
     with the Joint Writings of Henry Barrow
     and John Greenwood, ed. Leland H.
     Carlson, London: Allen & Unwin 1962,
     p.143.

34. Ibid., p.27. Greenwood, like Browne
     before him, was anxious not to be mis-
     taken for an anabaptist. In answer to the
     question, 'Do you hold it lawful to bap-
     tize children?' he replied, 'Yes, I am no
     Anabaptist, I thank God.' Ibid., p.26.

35. Ibid., p.98.

36. H.M.   Dexter,   op.cit.,   pp.402-410. P.T.
     Forsyth disagreed; see his Faith, Free-
     dom and the Future (1912), London: Inde-
     pendent Press, pp.169-70.

37. Quoted by A. Mackennal, The Evolution of
     Congregationalism,   London: Nisbet 1901,
     pp.77-8.

38. J. Robinson, A Just Separation (1610),
     Works, II, p.257.

39. J. Robinson, Of Religious Communion,
     Private and Public (1614), Works III,
     pp.106 ff.

40. J. Robinson, A Just and Necessary Apol-
     ogy of Certain Christians no less contu-
     meliously than commonly called Brownists
     or Barrowists, (1625), Works, III, p.14.

41. J. Robinson, A Treatise on the Lawful-
     ness of Hearing Ministers in the Church
     of England (1634, but written earlier),
     Works III, pp.363, 366-7, 374.

42. J. Robinson, Works, II, pp.110, 129, 132,
     137, 140, 141; III, p.13.

43. A Treatise on the Lawfulness, op.cit.,
     p.377.

44. A Just and Necessary Apology, op.cit.,
     p.79.

45. Daniel Neal, A History of the Puritans,
     abridged in two vols. by Edward Parsons,
     London 1811, I, p.371.

46. C. Burrage, op.cit., II, p.157. Cf. H.
     Jacob, An Attestation...That the Church

<u>government</u> ought to be always with the
<u>peoples</u> free consent. Also this, That a
<u>true Church under the Gospel</u> contayneth
<u>no more ordinary Congregations but one</u>,
1613.

47. See W. Walker, <u>op.cit</u>., pp.33 ff.

48. R.W. Dale, 'The Early Independents,' <u>Con-</u>
<u>gregational Union Jubilee Lectures,</u>
London: Hodder & Stoughton 1882, I p.45.
We turn a blind eye to his anachronistic
use of 'Congregational.' This name did
not come into <u>general</u> usage until 1641,
when William Kiffin wrote in <u>A Glimpse of</u>
<u>Sion's Glory</u> of 'a company of saints in a
Congregational way'; though the English
pastor at Flushing, John Wing, wrote in
his <u>A Collection of Sundry Matters</u> (1616)
that 'only the Congregational body pol-
itic spiritually independent, is Christ's
divine ordinance in the Gospel.' See C.
Burrage, <u>op.cit</u>., I p.315. The term 'Independency' likewise became current c.
1641, though its unhelpful implications
were noted as early as 1643 in <u>The Apolo-</u>
<u>geticall Narration</u>, as we shall see. 'In-
dependent' emphasised separation from an
unworthy Church and a hostile state;
'Congregational' was indicative of the
political basis of the saints. Gradually
the terms became used interchangeably
(and pejoratively) in England; in America
'Congregational' was the favoured term.

49. A. Mackennal, <u>Early Independents</u>, London:
CUEW 1893, p.124.

50. W.B. Selbie in <u>Mansfield College Essays</u>,
p.33.

51. R.W. Dale in _Essays and Addresses_, p.180.

                    CHAPTER THREE

1. Evidence that the transatlantic traffic
    was not all in one direction is provided
    by the careers of Samuel Eaton who, hav-
    ing made a notable contribution to early
    Congregationalism in Boston from 1637,
    returned to Lancashire and founded the
    first Congregational church in that coun-
    ty, at Dukinfield; and one of Cotton's
    students in Boston, Christopher Marshall,
    who left Boston for Yorkshire c.1643, and
    founded the first Congregational church
    in that county. So Bryan Dale in _PICC_ II
    1899, p.447; cf.Robert Halley, _Lanca-
    shire: Its Puritanism and Nonconformity_,
    Manchester 1869, I p.294; Bryan Dale,
    _Yorkshire Puritanism and Early Nonconfor-
    mity_, 1909 pp. 104-7.

2. R. Mather, _Church-Government and Church-
    Covenant Discussed_, 1643, p.9.

3. _An Apologeticall Narration_, p.3. Robert
    S. Paul's _The Assembly of the Lord: Pol-
    itics and Religion in the Westminster As-
    sembly and the 'Grand Debate'_, Edinburgh:
    T. & T. Clark 1985, has appeared since
    our text was completed.

4. _Ibid._, pp.11-12.

5. _Ibid._, pp.13-14.

6. _Ibid._, p.17.

7. _Ibid._, p.22.

8. <u>Ibid</u>., p.23.

9. <u>Ibid</u>., p.24. That not all were satisfied
    by this reply is clear from the <u>Anti-</u>
    <u>apologia</u> of Thomas Edwards (1644). He
    thought (p.197) that 'all the waters in
    the Thames will not wash ⌈the Indepen-
    dents⌉ from all just imputation of the
    names Independent and Brownist.'

10. See his <u>On the Constitution, Right, Or-</u>
    <u>der, and Government of the Churches of</u>
    <u>Christ</u>, <u>Works</u>, Edinburgh 1865, XI, Con-
    tents, Bk.V.

11. The full titles of Edwards's works are
    <u>Antiapologia: or, A Full Answer to the</u>
    <u>Apologeticall Narration of Mr. Goodwin,</u>
    <u>Mr. Nye, Mr. Sympson, Mr. Burroughs,</u>
    <u>Mr.Bridge, Members of the Assembly of</u>
    <u>Divines;</u> and <u>Gangraena: or a Catalogue</u>
    <u>and Discovery of Many of the Errours,</u>
    <u>Heresies, Blasphemies and Pernicious</u>
    <u>Practices of the Sectaries of this time,</u>
    <u>vented and acted in England in these last</u>
    <u>four years</u>. Burroughs's full titles are:
    <u>A Vindication of Mr. Burroughs, Against</u>
    <u>Mr. Edwards his foule Aspersions in his</u>
    <u>spreading Gangraena, and his Angry Anti-</u>
    <u>apologia. Concluding with a briefe De-</u>
    <u>claration of what the Independents would</u>
    <u>have;</u> and <u>Irenicum, to the Lovers of</u>
    <u>Truth and Peace</u>.

12. So C. Mather, <u>Ratio Disciplinae Fratrum</u>
    <u>Nov-Anglorum</u>, p.7; quoted by H.M. Dexter,
    <u>The Congregationalism of the Last Three</u>
    <u>Hundred Years, p.463</u>.

13. J. Cotton, <u>The Keyes of the Kingdom of</u>

Heaven, and Power thereof, <u>according to</u>
<u>the Word of God</u>, 1644, p.18.

14. <u>Ibid</u>., p.54.

15. John Cook, <u>What the Independents would</u>
<u>have, or, A Character, Declaring some of</u>
<u>their Tenets, and that desires to dis-</u>
<u>abuse those who speak ill of that they</u>
<u>know not</u>, 1647. Cook, a barrister of
Gray's Inn, conducted the prosecution of
Charles I.

16. <u>Ibid</u>., p.12.

17. W. Bartlett, $I\chi\nu o\gamma\rho\alpha\phi\iota\alpha$ or a <u>Model of the</u>
<u>Primitive Congregational Way</u>, 1647, chap.
II. <u>Rev</u>. xviii: 4 is among the texts on
which Bartlett draws for support.

18. <u>Ibid</u>., p.52: cf.J. Burroughes, <u>A Vindica-</u>
<u>tion</u>, p.22.

19. T. Hooker, <u>A Survey</u>, I pp.3, 14, 46.

20. <u>Ibid</u>., I, pp. 55 f.

21. <u>Ibid</u>., II, p.75. To some Congregationalists, however, the laying on of hands was
an unnecessary, and even a dangerously
sacerdotal ritual. To Bartlett (<u>op.cit</u>.,
p.107), as to the authors of the Savoy
<u>Declaration</u> (art.XII) the imposition of
hands was not a <u>sine qua non</u> of
ordination. Hooker himself (p.74) thought
that corporate prayer was the supremely
important thing. See further, G.F.
Nuttall, <u>Visible Saints</u>, pp.90-93; John
Huxtable, 'Ordination: Aspects of a
Tradition,' <u>The Journal of the United</u>

Reformed Church History Society, II no.4, 1979, pp.94-106.

22. Ibid., II, pp.79-80.

23. Ibid., IV, p.1.

24. S. Ford, A Gospel-Church, or God's Holy Temple Opened, 1675, p.6.

25. I. Chauncy, The Divine Institution of Congregational Churches, Ministry and Ordinances...Asserted and Proved from the Word of God, 1697, pp.2,3,4,6,7,12, 13,23,30,34,134.

26. J. Owen, The Duty of Pastors and People Distinguished (1644), Works ed. W.H. Goold, 1850-53, XIII, p.5. Owen's Works were reprinted by the Banner of Truth Trust, 1965 ff.

27. J. Owen, Eschol; or Rules of Direction for the Walking of the Saints in Fellowship according to the Order of the Gospel (1648), Works XIII, pp.68-9. He refers to II Cor. vi:14 ff and Rev. xviii:4.

28. See his A Vindication of the Treatise about the Nature of Schism (1657), Works XIII, pp. 223 ff.

29. Daniel Cawdrey, Independencie a Great Schism, 1657, p.88.

30. J. Owen, Of Schism (1657), Works XIII, pp.175 ff; cf. his 'To the Reader' prefaced to Eschol.

31. These are two of the chapter headings in

Owen, <u>An Inquiry into the Original Nature ...and Communion of Evangelical Churches</u> (1681), <u>Works</u> XV.

32. J. Owen, <u>The True Nature of a Gospel Church and Its Government</u> (1689), <u>Works</u> XVI, p.12.

33. <u>Ibid</u>., p.13.

34. <u>Ibid</u>., p.25.

35. <u>Ibid</u>., p.31.

36. <u>Ibid</u>., p.36.

37. <u>Ibid</u>., p.37.

38. <u>Ibid</u>., p.185.

39. <u>Ibid</u>., p.196.

40. <u>Ibid</u>., p.205.

41. <u>Ibid</u>., p. 208.

42. J. Owen, Sermon XXI, 'Gospel Charity,' on Col.iii:14, Works IX, p.262.

43. W. Walker, <u>The Creeds and Platforms of Congregationalism</u>, p.116.

44. <u>Ibid</u>., pp.116-117. The covenant was renewed yet again in 1660-61, when the members cautioned themselves against a leaven of Quakerism (p.118). Cf. the 'cheerfully subscribed' Agreement (1656) of the ministers of Cumberland and Westmorland, in which they attribute the considerable Quaker presence in their area to the fact

that 'Satan is enraged,' and hence the Quakers 'come upon us like a furious Torrent.' See Francis Nicholson and Ernest Axon, <u>The Older Nonconformity in Kendal</u>, Kendal, Titus Wilson, 1915, p.27.

45. See A.J. Grieve and W. Marshall Jones, <u>These Three Hundred Years</u>, London: Independent Press 1946, p.20.

46. <u>Ibid</u>., pp.21-22.

47. Although this church was variously designated 'Congregational' and 'Presbyterian,' its government was congregational from the first.

48. In the edition of the Savoy <u>Declaration</u> by A.G. Matthews (London: Independent Press 1959) the amendments and additions to the <u>Westminster Confession</u> made by the Savoy fathers are printed in heavy type. In 1680 the Massachussetts Synod made slight amendments to the <u>Declaration</u>, and the whole was reproduced, furnished with proof texts, as the <u>Saybrook Platform</u> of 1708. In a speech to the Protector Thomas Goodwin made it clear that the main purpose of the Savoy Conference was to clear the Congregationalists of the charge that 'Independentism (as they call it) is the sink of all Heresies and Schisms.' See A.G. Matthews, <u>op.cit</u>., p.12.

49. W. Walker, <u>op.cit</u>., p.203.

50. A.G. Matthews, <u>op.cit</u>., p.121.

51. W. Walker, <u>op.cit</u>., p.205.

52. Ibid., pp.205-6.

53. Ibid., p.207.

54. A.G. Matthews, op.cit., p.122.

55. Ibid.

56. W. Walker, op.cit., p.212.

57. Ibid., p.212 n.1.

58. Ibid., p.461.

59. A.G. Matthews, op.cit., pp.126-7.

60. W. Walker, op.cit., pp.229-234.

CHAPTER FOUR

1. G.F. Nuttall, Visible Saints, p.viii.

2. The classic debates on this point are
    those between John Howe and Bishops Ward
    and Stillingfleet. See Henry Rogers, The
    Life and Character of John Howe, M.A.,
    2nd edn. (1862) p.87; Howe's Works, ed.
    H. Rogers, 1873; and the reference in our
    final chapter below.

3. See e.g. W. Gordon Robinson, 'Congrega-
    tionalism and the Historic Faith,' CQ
    XXIX 1951, pp.202-213; G.F. Nuttall,
    Congregationalists and Creeds, London:
    Epworth [1966].

4. J. Owen, The True Nature of a Gospel
    Church, Works XVI, p.171.

5. A. Mackennal, Early Independents, p.139.

6.   Quoted by N. Micklem, God's Freemen, London: James Clarke [1922], pp.147-8.

7.   Quoted by R.W. Dale, 'The Early Independents,' Congregational Union Jubilee Lectures, I. p.25.

8.   J. Burroughes, Irenicum, p.41.

9.   See J. Goodwin, Θεομαχια, 1644.

10. See From Uniformity to Unity, 1662-1962, ed. G.F. Nuttall and Owen Chadwick, London: Epworth 1962, pp.172-3; G.F. Nuttall, 'Assembly and Association in Dissent, 1689-1831,' in Councils and Assemblies, Studies in Church History VII, ed. G.J. Cuming and Derek Baker, Cambridge: CUP 1971, p.295.

11. Dr. William's Library mss. 12.78.13.

12. The Note Book of Thomas Jolly, ed. Henry Fishwick, Manchester: Chetham Society 1895, p.42.

13. Allan Brockett, Nonconformity in Exeter, 1650-1875, Manchester:Manchester UP 1962, pp.29-30.

14. Quoted by A. Peel, These Hundred Years, London: CUEW [1931] p.6.

15. See G.F. Nuttall, 'Assembly and Association in Dissent,' op.cit., p.309, referring to A.R. Henderson, History of Castle Gate Congregational Church, Nottingham, 1655-1905, London: James Clarke 1905, chap. VIII; Reginald Mansfield, The Development of Independency in Derbyshire,

unpublished doctoral dissertation, University of Manchester 1951, pp.108-113.

16. R.Bragge, Church Discipline, 1739, pp.7,8.

17. Howell Harris's Visits to Pembrokeshire, transcribed by Tom Beynon, Aberystwyth: The Cambrian News Press 1966, p.65.

18. See A.P.F. Sell, Church Planting: A Case Study of Westmorland Nonconformity, Worthing: Henry E. Walter, 1986, p.76.

19. Cotton Mather, Ratio Disciplinae Fratrum Nov-Anglorum, A Faithful Account of the Discipline Professed and Practised in the Churches of New England, Boston 1726, p.3.

20. W. Walker, The Creeds and Platforms of Congregationalism, chap.XV.

21. C. Mather, op.cit., p.181.

22. Hussey's work is God's Operations of Grace But No Offers of Grace (1707), abridged edn., Primitive Press, Elon College, N.C., 1973. For a fuller discussion of the matters thus far raised in this paragraph see A.P.F. Sell, The Great Debate: Calvinism, Arminianism and Salvation, Worthing: Henry E. Walter, 1982, Grand Rapids: Baker Book House, 1983.

23. W. Gordon Robinson, A History of the Lancashire Congregational Union, 1806-1956, Manchester: Lancashire Congregational Union 1955, p.23.

24. M. Maurice, Social Religion Exemplify'd, 1750, p.305.

25. *Ibid*., p.325.

26. W.G. Robinson, *op.cit*., p.23.

27. For the text of the propositions see F.J. Powicke, <u>A History of the Cheshire County Union of Congregational Churches</u>, Manchester: Griffiths 1907, pp.21-22.

28. W.G. Robinson, *op.cit*., p.25.

29. *Ibid*., p.28.

30. For the difference in atmosphere between earlier and later Associations see G.F. Nuttall, *art.cit*., p.304.

31. The story of the Union's formation and first hundred years is told by A. Peel, <u>These Hundred Years</u>: cf. J. Stoughton, <u>Reminiscences of Congregationalism Fifty Years Ago</u>, London: Hodder & Stoughton 1881, pp.18-22 for an insight into motives on either side of the Union debate.

32. It is interesting to note that whereas the English movement was fathered largely by the evangelical spirit, the founders of the National Council of Congregational Churches (1871) in America were so exercised by organisational considerations that the topic of evangelism did not appear in Council discussions for the next thirty-six years. See G.G. Atkins and F.L. Fagley, <u>History of American Congregationalism</u>, p.272.

33. See R.T. Jenkins, 'Yr Annibynwyr Cymreig a Hywel Harris,' <u>Cofiadur</u> XII, 1935, pp.28,30; cf. G.F. Nuttall, <u>Howel Harris,</u>

1714-1772, The Last Enthusiast, Cardiff: U. Wales Press 1965, p.45; 'The students of Trevecca College 1768-1791,' Cymmrodorian Society Transactions, July 1968; The Significance of Trevecca Col- lege 1768-1791, London: Epworth 1969; 'Calvinism in Free Church History,' The Baptist Quarterly XXII 1968, pp.418-428.

34. See G.F. Nuttall, Howel Harris, pp.45-46. For Grey see Dictionary of Welsh Biography, ed. Sir John Lloyd and R.T. Jenkins, 1959.

35. See G.F. Nuttall, Calendar of the Correspondence of Philip Doddridge DD (1702-1751), London: HMSO 1979, pp.149, 181, 186.

36. 'Memoir of the Late Rev. Richard Morgan, Henllan Amgoed, Carms.,' The London Christian Instructor, or Congregational Magazine, IV 1821, pp.338-9.

CHAPTER FIVE

1. The complete document was printed in full in CYB from 1846-1917. To the American Williston Walker it was 'a sweet-spirited statement of which the English churches have no cause to be ashamed.' Quoted by A.J. Grieve in Congregationalism Through the Centuries, London: Independent Press 1937, p.94.

2. CYB 1866, p.xii.

3. Among theological contrasts may be noted Savoy's objectivist sacramental doctrine,

and the _Declaration's_ subjectivist emphasis. The Romantic movement and Zwingli
were unconscious allies here.

4. A. Peel, _These Hundred Years_, p.3.

5. Albert J. Lyman, 'Independence and Fellowship,' _PICC_ II, 1899, p.436.

6. Quoted by W. Gordon Robinson, _William
   Roby_, London: Independent Press 1954,
   p.44.

7. _The Christian's Penny Magazine_ I, 1846,
   p.62.

8. _Ibid._, p.35.

9. _Ibid._, p.36.

10. 'W', 'Congregationalism in 1850,' _The
    Evangelical Magazine_, N.S. XXVIII, 1850,
    p.175.

11. T. Witherow's book (1856) is still in
    print: Free Presbyterian Publications,
    Glasgow. The full title of Dexter's work
    is, _Congregationalism: What it is; Whence
    it is; How it works; Why it is better
    than any other form of church-government;
    and its consequent demands_, Boston 1874.

12. Dugald Macfadyen, _Constructive Congrega-
    tional Ideals_, London: Allenson 1902,
    pp.9-10.

13. G.B. Johnson, _Our Principles_, London:
    Hodder & Stoughton, 3rd edn. 1868, p.36.

14. H.M. Dexter, _The Congregationalism of the_

Last Three Hundred Years, p.714.

15. 'Congregationalism,' _The Congregation-alist_ I, Jan. 1872, p.6. Dale was editor at the time and contributed this editorial.

16. See _CYB_ 1883.

17. _CYB_ 1898, p.33.

18. R.W. Dale, _The Pilgrim Fathers_, London: Hamilton, Adams 1854, p.13.

19. R. W. Dale, 'The Divine Life in Man,' _PICC_ I, 1891, p.38.

20. In D. Macfadyen, _op.cit._, p.136. Such an experience, though never received without wonder and thanksgiving, ought to be normal.

21. J. Vernon Bartlet, 'Congregationalism, Essential and Relative,' in _Essays Congregational and Catholic_, p.45.

22. B.L. Manning, _Why Not Abandon the Church?_ London: Independent Press 1939, pp.37-38.

23. D. Macfadyen, _op.cit._, p.36.

24. _Ibid._, p.229.

25. _Ibid._, pp.275,13.

26. E.g. at the third Assembly of the ICC. See _PICC_ III, 1908, p.269; cf. W.B. Selbie, _Congregationalism_, London:Methuen 1927, p.12; and many others.

27. A. Peel, <u>Inevitable Congregationalism,</u> London: Independent Press 1937, p.70.

28. On this point see H.F. Lovell Cocks, 'Where Two or Three,' <u>World Congregation-alism</u> III no.8, 1961, pp. 33-34.

29. W.G. Robinson, <u>William Roby</u>, p.48.

30. <u>Congregationalism</u>, a statement by repre-sentatives of the CUEW to the Faith and Order department of the World Council of Churches, 1951, p.18. And the CUEW pam-phlet, <u>Church Membership</u> (1949), on which many of those reading this study may have been reared, reviews the history briefly, and concludes: 'Out of this long contro-versy certain principles have been made clear which Congregationalists believe to be fundamental as constituting the Church:-1. The Church is not something that men have made, but it exists because of something which God has done. It is God in Christ Who creates the Church. 2. The Church is constituted of Christian men and women who have made their response to God's call. 3. Wherever Christians gather, realizing the Presence of Christ, and submitting themselves in obedience to Him, there is the Church. 4. To such a Church Christ gives power and competence to do His Will. 5. The rule of faith in the Church thus conceived is the Bible interpreted by the Holy Spirit.' <u>Op.cit</u>., pp.13-14.

31. S.T. Porter, <u>Lectures of the Ecclesias-tical System of the Independents,</u> Glasgow: Maclehose 1856, p.178.

32. The London Christian Instructor, or Congregational Magazine, VII 1824, p.240.

33. J. Stoughton, Reminiscences, pp.71-72.

34. Anon, Brief Notes on Some Present Questions Affecting Independency, London: William & Norgate 1871, pp.15-16.

35. The Congregationalist I, 1872, p.6.

36. R.W. Dale, History of English Congregationalism, London: Hodder & Stoughton 1907, pp.374-5. T.W. Manson was later to add what he regarded as the missing principle: 'By the will of Christ every Christian Church has an obligation to care for and be in fellowship with other Christian Churches.' See his The Church's Ministry, London: Hodder & Stoughton 1948, p.94.

37. M. Caston, Independency in Bristol, 1860, p.37.

38. A.W.W. Dale, The Life of R.W. Dale, London: Hodder & Stoughton 1899, p.243. Cf. D.W. Simon's letter to James Ross in F.J. Powicke, David Worthington Simon, London: Hodder & Stoughton 1912, pp. 246-7. Cf. R. Mackintosh, 'The Genius of Congregationalism,' in Essays Congregational and Catholic, p.107: 'The North of England saint, who prefers Congregationalism to other polities because he "likes to have his say" in Church matters, is very little of a Congregationalist and hardly anything at all of a Christian.' See also PICC IV, 1920, p.392, and William Hewgill, 'The Confession of a

County Union Secretary,' in ed. D.
Macfadyen, op.cit., p.203: 'There are
still men who make a fetish of their
so-called Independency. They are idola-
ters of a name.' In the 1940s the
Lancashire Union published a pamphlet in
which the rights of the local church were
emphasized.

39. R.W. Dale, Essays and Addresses, p.158.

40. CYB, 1897.

41. PICC I, 1891, pp.202,203.

42. PICC II, 1899, p.443.

43. B. Nightingale, Congregationalism Reexamined, London: CUEW 1918, p.18. This pamphlet was a reply to A. Peel, The Congregational Principle, London: James Clarke,
1917.

44. P.T. Forsyth, Congregationalism and Re-
union, London: Independent Press 1952,
p.46. Cf. J.D. Jones, 'Catholic Independency,' CYB 1910, p.41: 'autonomy is not
the first thing; spirituality is the
first and essential thing.'

45. A. Peel, Inevitable Congregationalism,
pp.73-74.

46. E.g. PICC III, 1908, p.300.

47. A. Pringle, 'The Two Independencies,' CQ
I, 1923, p.157.

48. N. Micklem, Congregationalism and the
Church Catholic, London: Independent Press

1943, p.29. We presume it was a slip of
the pen that enabled Dr. Micklem to speak
of the independency of the <u>congregation</u>
as being a Congregational principle.

49. 'Congregational and Presbyterian Systems,' an article transcribed from <u>The
New Englander</u> in <u>The Congregational Maga-
zine</u>, N.S. IX 1845, p.703. The Czar, as
is well known, has latterly fallen.
Whether erstwhile Presbyterians now in
the United Reformed Church consider that
their old church order is similarly sunk
without trace is not known! It is not, of
course.

50. <u>The Autobiography of William Jay</u> (1854),
Edinburgh: The Banner of Truth Trust
1974, pp.167-8.

51. Quoted by J. Stoughton, <u>op.cit</u>., p.60.

52. See his Annual Address to the CUEW, <u>CYB</u>
1851, p.71.

53. <u>CYB</u> 1853, pp.10,11.

54. <u>CYB</u> 1856, p.8.

55. <u>CYB</u> 1862, p.47.

56. <u>Ibid</u>., p.58.

57. Alexander Mackennal, <u>Life of John Allison
Macfadyen, M.A., D.D.</u>, London: Hodder &
Stoughton 1891, p.91.

58. See his <u>Congregational Independency in
Contradistinction to Episcopacy and Presbyterianism: the Church Polity of the New</u>

Testament, Glasgow: Maclehose 1864, chap. VIII.

59. CYB 1880, p.69.

60. PICC I, p.146.

61. Ibid., our italics. The view of the Church as the extension of the incarnation was challenged by some Congregationalists, and notably by P.T. Forsyth in The Church and the Sacraments (1917), London: Independent Press 1953, p.83: 'That which owes itself to a rebirth cannot be a prolongation of the ever sinless...The Church is not the continuation of Christ, but His creation and His response.'

62. CYB 1882, p.60.

63. Ibid., p.63.

64. Quoted by A. Peel, Inevitable Congregationalism, p.91.

65. CYB 1902, p.24. The matter is judiciously probed by John H.Taylor, 'Joseph Parker's United Congregational Church,' CHST XIX, 1961 pp.91-96.

66. Ibid., p.26.

67. E.g. J.W.G. Dew, 'Congregationalism Today and Tomorrow,' CQ XIII 1935, p.450.

68. N. Micklem, op.cit., p.33.

69. In an address on 'The Congregational Tradition,' delivered at Carrs Lane church

church Birmingham on 1st June 1948; quoted by Charles E. Surman, <u>Alexander James Grieve, M.A.,D.D.</u>, Manchester: Lancashire Independent College 1953, p.47. On this matter Bernard Lord Manning was with Dr. Grieve. See his <u>Essays in Orthodox Dissent</u>, London: Independent Press 1953, p.157.

70. <u>PICC</u> VI, 1949, p.38.

71. H.F.Lovell Cocks, 'Congregational Church-manship,' <u>PICC</u> VII 1953, p.52.

72. Leslie E. Cooke, PICC VII, p.86. We place the term 'administrators' in inverted commas by way of suggesting that Dr. Cooke, and many others like him, were so much more than that. At the same time it has to be said that Congregationalism has never had an adequate theory to cover ministers who are not local pastors. Historically, many pastors were non-stipendiary. Today some stipendiary ministers are not local pastors, while a number of ministers are neither stipendiaries nor local pastors.

73. See A. Mackennal, <u>Sketches in the Evolution of English Congregationalism,</u> pp. 190,192,212,220.

74. 'T', 'The Advantages of Independency,' <u>The London Christian Instructor</u>, IV 1821, p.576.

75. See <u>CYB</u> 1898: Berry's Autumnal Address to the Union.

76. See Macfadyen's Annual Address to the

Union, <u>CYB</u> 1883. Does one's suspicion that many members of the United Reformed Church would be surprised - even horrified - to think of a great conflict impending as between the URC and Rome indicate either that major doctrinal rapprochment has occurred since Macfadyen's day, or that either Rome, the URC or both are doctrinally apathetic? It certainly suggests that the parties are friendlier than they used to be, and this is all to the good. We may note in passing that Congegationalism's high doctrine of the Church was employed in the discussion of the establishment question. See e.g. <u>Mansfield College Essays</u>, p.35.

77. P.T. Forsyth, <u>Faith, Freedom and the Future</u>, p.215.

78. <u>CYB</u> 1882, p.54.

79. <u>PICC</u> I, p.137.

80. A.M. Fairbairn, <u>The Place of Christ in Modern Theology</u>, London: Hodder&Stoughton 6th edn. 1894, p.529.

81. <u>PICC</u> VI, p.2. This position was advocated in detail by P.T. Forsyth in <u>The Church and the Sacraments</u>, see especially chap. III. See also Glynmor John, <u>Congregationalism in an Ecumenical Era</u>, London: Independent Press 1967.

82. See e.g. A.P.F. Sell, <u>Theology in Turmoil: The roots, course and significance of the conservative-liberal debate in modern theology</u>, Grand Rapids: Baker Book House, 1986, chap.II.

83. For Forsyth's characteristically blunt dismissal of this stance see his Congregationalism and Reunion, p.63.

84. Quoted by A. Peel, These Hundred Years, p.56.

85. Quoted by J. Stoughton, op.cit., p.69; cf. The London Christian Instructor, IV 1821, p.574.

86. CYB 1854, p.14.

87. The Autobiography of William Jay, pp. 166-7.

88. See the titles of their books at notes 58 and 11 above.

89. See e.g. H. Allon, CYB 1882, p.55. Cf.D. Macfadyen's use of Hort in Constructive Congregational Ideals, pp.292-4. By 1909 W.B. Selbie can add Sanday and Gwatkin to the list of supportive Anglicans. See Mansfield College Essays, p.24; cf. B. Nightingale, op.cit., p.15; J.V. Bartlet in Essays Congregational and Catholic, p.42.

90. Quoted by C.E. Surman, op.cit., p.48.

91. R.W. Dale in Congregational Union Jubilee Lectures, I, p.39 (our ital.)

92. PICC III 1908, p.266.

93. J. Stoughton, op.cit., p.89; cf. A. Mackennal, J.A. Macfadyen, p.193.

94. F.J. Powicke, Essentials of Congregation-

alism, London: James Clarke 1899, p.51.

95. E.g. his _Essays and Addresses_, p.117. Cf.
    The Congregationalist I, 1872, p.4, where
    he argues that even two or three
    Patterdale shepherds could, provided they
    were regenerate, constitute a church.

96. _PICC_ IV, 1920, pp.393,478.

97. _PICC_ I, p.203.

98. N. Micklem, _Congregationalism Today_,
    London: Hodder & Stoughton 1937, pp.7,11.
    See his _The Box and the Puppets_, London:
    Bles 1957, pp.93-99 for the 'manifesto'
    of the group, which included _inter alia_
    John Whale, Bernard Manning and Micklem
    himself.

99. A.J.B. Higgins, 'The Doctrine of the
    Church in Congregationalism,' _CQ_ XXIV,
    1946, p.132. Professor Higgins is now an
    Anglican.

100. D. Jenkins, _Congregationalism: A Restate-
     ment_, London: Faber 1954, pp.71-2. The
     context of Dr. Jenkins' discussion -
     church order - must be borne in mind.
     Clearly there are Reformed Churches which
     require confessional assent on the part
     of their ministers; and which maintain
     the establishment principle. Congrega-
     tionalism does neither. Cf. D. Jenkins,
     The Church Meeting and Democracy, London:
     Independent Press 1944, pp.22 ff.

101. B.L. Manning, _Essays in Orthodox Dissent_,
     p.117.

102. J. Huxtable, 'God's Sovereignty over the Church,' in _Christian Confidence_, ed.F.R. Tomes, London: SPCK 1970, p.124.

103. W.G. Robinson, 'Congregationalism and the Historic Faith,' _CQ_ XXIX, 1951, p.213.

104. _The London Christian Instructor_ IV, 1821, p.575 n. Contrast H.M. Dexter, _Congregationalism_ p.5. where the polity is allowed to a number of other groups.

105. _CYB_ 1854, p.55.

106. T.M. Herbert in _Religious Republics: Six Essays on Congregationalism_, London: Longmans 1869, p.81.

107. G.G. Atkins and F.L. Fagley, _op.cit._, pp.319-320.

108. See his _Manual of Congregational Principles_, London: Hodder & Stoughton 1884, pp.186-8.

109. Quoted in A.W.W. Dale, _op.cit._, p.345.

110. _The Congregationalist_ I 1872, p.3.

111. A quotation from his Chairman's Address of 1879; see A.Mackennal, _J.A. Macfadyen_, p.179.

112. Quoted by H.S.J. Guntrip, _Smith and Wrigley of Leeds_, London: Independent Press 1944, pp.120-121. For the wider story see A.P.F. Sell, '_Theology in Turmoil_.

113. F. Wrigley, _Congregationalism and the_

Church Meeting, London: CUEW n.d., p.158 (but vol.X of a series of small, consecutively numbered pamphlets under the general heading, Faith and Conduct: Papers for Young People).

114. F.J. Powicke, D.W. Simon, p.246, quoting a letter to James Ross dated 22.4.1904.

115. So F.J. Powicke, Ibid, p.221.

116. Ibid., p.231.

117. PICC III, 1908, p.116.

118. P.T. Forsyth, The Principle of Authority (1913), London: Independent Press 1952, p.249; cf. his Faith, Freedom and the Future, pp.189-90, 224, 293, 339, 347.

119. C.J. Cadoux, The Congregational Way, Oxford: Blackwell 1945, pp.23-4.

120. PICC VII, 1953, pp.47,49.

121. H.M. Dexter, The Congregationalism of the last Three Hundred Years as seen in its Literature, p.711.

122. See A. Peel and Douglas Horton, International Congregationalism, London: Independent Press 1949.

CHAPTER SIX

1. PICC II, 1899, p.448.

2. Short Tracts for the Times on Church Principles, No.12, CUEW, n.d., p.3.

3. The Distinctive Principles of Congrega-
    tional Polity, n.d., p.4.

4. Quoted by A.Peel, Inevitable Congrega-
    tionalism, pp.91-92.

5. Ralph Wardlaw, Congregational Independ-
    ency, Glasgow: Maclehose 1864, pp.49-92.

6. Among these see e.g. G.B. Johnson, Our
    Principles, London: Hodder & Stoughton
    1868, pp.31-34; R.W. Dale, A Manual, pp.
    212-213; Albert Goodrich, A Primer of
    Congregationalism, London: CUEW 1902.
    Later works in the same genre include
    E.J. Price, A Handbook of Congregation-
    alism, London: CUEW 1924; A.D. Martin,
    Principles of the Congregational
    Churches, London: CUEW 1927; John Marsh,
    For the Church Member, London: Independ-
    ent Press 1946. During the 1950s the
    Life and Work Department of the CUEW pub-
    lished a series of pamphlets under the
    general title The Church and the Kingdom.
    The series included The Sacrament of Bap-
    tism, The Meaning of the Communion Ser-
    vice, Church Membership, The High Calling
    and Work of a Deacon, Our Heritage of
    Free Prayer, etc.

7. The Congregationalist II, 1873, p.330.

8. Quoted by D. Macfadyen, Constructive Con-
    gregational Ideals, p.211.

9. Quoted by W.B. Selbie, The Life of Andrew
    Martin Fairbairn, London:Hodder&Stoughton
    1914, p.157.

10. J.S. Griffith, CQ XVII, 1939, pp.189 ff.

11. C.J. Cadoux,'Congregationalism the True Catholicism,' in _Essays Congregational and Catholic_, pp.69,74.

12. C.J. Cadoux, _The Congregational Way_, p.19.

13. Lancashire Union _Report_, n.d. but 1940s, p.4.

14. N. Micklem, _Congregationalism and the Church Catholic_, London: Independent Press 1943, pp.50-52.

15. G.F. Nuttall, 'Presbyterian-Congregational Union? - I wonder?' _CQ_ XXV 1947, p.303.

16. E. Routley, _Congregationalists and Unity_, London: Mowbray 1962, p.32.

17. See his Introduction to J. Owen, _The True Nature of a Gospel Church_, London: James Clarke 1947, p.21.

18. D. Jenkins, _Congregationalism: A Restatement_, p.84. Eleven years earlier R.K. Orchard had entered a powerful plea for a theological understanding by Congregationalists of church councils. See his, 'The Place of Church Councils in Congregationalism,' in John Marsh (ed.), _Congregationalism Today_, London: Independent Press 1943, pp.71-101.

19. Few have been as adept as Dr. Lovell Cocks at the impish purveying of home truths. In a sermon preached at Argyle church, Bath to the Congregational Council in 1972, he said: 'Listen to this rule of the Congregational Union - you'll find in the Year Book for 1912 or there-

abouts: "In the interest of the Aided
Churches it is required as an absolute
condition of grant that no invitation be
given to any person to accept the pastorate, or even to supply the pulpit with a
view to the pastorate, without the ap-
proval of the Executive of the County
Union." You won't find anything in the
Scheme of Union half as grimly peremptory
as that! What has happened to the absolute autonomy of the two or three gathered in Christ's name? Some churches it
seems are more independent than others.
Absolute autonomy costs more money than
our aided churches can afford. If independence means financial dependency, then
anyone looking for New Testament warrant
for that won't find it – though he seek
it diligently and with tears.' From a
duplicated copy of the sermon, p.2.

20. G.B. Caird, 'Church (Ekklesia) in the New
Testament,' a supplementary pamphlet to
Commission I's Report. Continuing Congregationalists are to be found in the Evangelical Fellowship of Congregational
Churches (1966) and the Congregational
Federation (1972). For the latter group
see R.W. Cleaves, The Story of the Federation. Sadly, the opening page of Mr.
Cleaves's Introduction is needlessly
shrill. It is not true to say, for example, that for those Congregationalists
who entered the United Reformed Church
'Historic Independency no longer mattered
and was thrown to the wind.' Likewise the
Scroll of the Congregational Federation
refers to those who, at union with the
Presbyterians, 'deemed it right for them
to forsake the Congregational Way' (p.79).

This is not, of course, what they themselves thought they were doing; and we
shall suggest that the marks of visible
sainthood, orderliness and catholicity,
which ever characterised Congregationalism at its best have been incorporated
into the Basis of Union of the United
Reformed Church, and that they now help
to inform a corporate episcopacy of the
most mutual, though not of the merely
expedient, kind. Harold Hodgkins's
statement of <u>The Congregational Way:</u>
<u>Apostolic legacy, ministry, unity, free-</u>
<u>dom</u> was published by the Congregational
Federation, Nottingham, 1982. Commended
by F.F. Bruce it was adversely reviewed
by Stephen H. Mayor in <u>The Journal of the</u>
<u>United Reformed Church History Society</u>
<u>III</u> no.1, 1983, p.36. Similar discussion
had been taking place in America where,
in 1957, nearly one tenth of all Congregationalists remained outside the United
Church of Christ, which was formed by the
union of Congregationalists with those of
the Evangelical and Reformed Church. See
e.g. Harold N. Skidmore, 'Last Stages of
the Merger,' <u>The Christian World</u>, 6.7.
1961, p.5; Henry David Gray, 'Against the
Merger,' <u>ibid</u>., 24.8.1961, p.5; Harland
G.Lewis, 'The United Church of Christ in
the U.S.A.,' <u>World Congregationalism</u> III
no.9, 1961, pp.3-9; Harry R. Butman,
'Look to the Rock,' <u>ibid</u>., IV no.11,
1962, pp.35-39; Henry David Gray, <u>The</u>
<u>Mediators</u>, Ventura, California: American
Congregational Center, 1984.

21.   J. Huxtable, <u>PICC</u> X, 1966, p.33.

22. The present writer shared early bewilder-
     ment as witness his 'Commission I: From
     the Camp of the Bewildered,' The Chris-
     tian World, 9.11.1961, p.8. Later, after
     desired clarification had been offered,
     he and some others concluded that no com-
     promise of vital principle had occurred.
     See our letter to the editor of The Con-
     gregational Monthly, July 1969, p.14.

23. Not the least difficulty faced by those
     who advocated a national covenant was the
     fact that since the late eighteenth-cen-
     tury when, as we have seen, anti-Unitari-
     an covenants were adopted, the idea of
     local covenants had slipped from view.
     Certainly the nineteenth-century manuals
     do not dwell upon the idea. A fortiori a
     national covenant seemed to some to be a
     dangerously novel notion. Cf. W. Gordon
     Robinson, 'Covenant Relationship. Its
     History in Congregationalism,' The Chris-
     tian World, 8.6.1961. For a concise
     statement of the pro-covenant case see
     W.J.F. Huxtable in World Congregational-
     ism, III no.9. September 1961, pp.11-14.

24. Oversight and Covenant. Interim Report of
     Commission No.I. Some Questions and
     Answers, London: CUEW n.d., Q & A 6. Cf.
     Douglas Horton's Introduction to the 1960
     edn. of W. Walker, The Creeds and Plat-
     forms of Congregationalism, pp.viii-ix.

25. CYB 1966-67, p.41.

26. Declaration, p.34.

27. Interim Report of Commission I, p.6.

28. In his generally useful account of the
     formation of the United Reformed Church
     Hubert Smith does not give due weight to
     this point. See his unpublished M. Phil.
     thesis, University of London 1977, <u>The
     Formation of the United Reformed Church:
     A Theological and Sociological Elucida-
     tion</u>.

29. The following (slightly abbreviated) are
     the relevant clauses of the <u>Basis of
     Union</u>:
     (1) There is but one Church of the one
         God. He called Israel to be his peo-
         ple, and in fulfilment of the purpose
         then begun he called the Church into
         being through Jesus Christ, by the
         power of the Holy Spirit.
     (2) The one Church of the one God is
         holy...because there Christ dwells
         with his people.
     (3) The Church is catholic or universal
         because Christ calls into it all peo-
         ples and because it proclaims the
         fullness of Christ's gospel to all
         men.
     (4) The Church is apostolic because
         Christ continues to entrust it with
         the gospel and the commission first
         given to the apostles to proclaim
         that gospel to all peoples.
     (16) The United Reformed Church gives
         thanks for the common life of the
         Church, wherein the people of God,
         being made members one of another,
         are called to love and serve one
         another and all men and to grow to-
         gether in grace and in the knowledge
         of the Lord Jesus Christ. Participat-
         ing in the common life of the Church

within the local church, they enter
into the life of the Church throughout the world...

30. Baptism, a Statement prepared by the
Theological Group of the CUEW, London:
Independent Press [1962] p.10. Contrast
F.J. Powicke, 'The Congregational
Churches,' in Evangelical Christianity,
ed.W.B. Selbie, London: Hodder&Stoughton
[1911], p.105: 'It is also to the good that
Baptism is not now confined to the
children of believing parents - one or
both. For that is a change due to escape
from the Calvinistic conception of a lim-
ited covenant - a covenant for the elect
only - to the conception of a grace,
which is in covenant, or saving relation,
to all mankind. It is a change which can
do justice to the words "of such is the
Kingdom of Heaven," and so claims every
child for God.' (But is it not one thing
to take Jesus as teaching the need of
child-likeness on the part of members of
the Kingdom, and quite another to suggest
that his words have anything to do with
Baptism? And in so far as Jesus welcomed
the child, do not churches do this every
Sunday?) Powicke was echoing Dr. Eustace
Conder, who welcomed the fact that 'the
wider view and practice have come to be
generally accepted among us, that children who are placed under Christian
teaching and training should be admitted
to Baptism, even though their parents be
not godly persons.' See Congregational
Union Tracts on Church Principles (formerly called Leeds Tracts), No.3[1885],
p.8. But the first of the Second Series
of Congregational Union Tracts, Baptism

(1863), does not contemplate the baptism of children whose parents do not profess the Christian faith.

In this paragraph 'joining' or 'becoming a member of' the Church mean 'completing one's Christian initiation begun at baptism by profession of faith and enrolment.' For the latter a degree of 'saintly' maturity is required - especially given the responsibilities of the church meeting. In recent years there has been a tendency for young people to make their profession in their early teens. In this case they need positive encouragement to fulfil their church meeting responsibilities as soon as appropriate; and Church meetings, related as they are to the worship of the church, need to be occasions on which the Word received in preaching and sacrament is applied in mission and service by the saints where God has placed them.

31. Though see now Alan Sell, <u>Church Discipline</u>, London: United Reformed Church 1983: a pamphlet written for the Doctrine and Worship Committee of the United Reformed Church.

32. Robert Baillie, <u>A Dissuasive from the Errours of the Time</u>, 1645, p.93.

33. J. Howe in his reply to Bishop Stillingfleet's 'Sermon of Schism,' <u>Works</u> ed. H. Rogers, 1873, V pp.232,257.

34. A.M. Fairbairn, <u>Catholicism, Roman and Anglican</u>, London: Hodder & Stoughton, 2nd edn. 1899, p.348.

Descriptive
Index of Persons

Abbreviations:

Ch.	Chairman
CM	Congregational minister
CCEW	Congregational Church in England & Wales
CUEW	Congregational Union of England & Wales
LMS	London Missionary Society
Mod.GA	Moderator of the General Assembly
URC	United Reformed Church
WCC	World Council of Churches

Where possible the scene of a person's main ministry is given.